America Needs a Sweeping Tax Revolution!

- The federal tax bite has risen more than tenfold since 1950, when only 2 percent of the average person's earnings went to income taxes.
- Family exemptions have been cut down to almost nothing by inflation.
- The IRS destroys our privacy and abuses honest taxpayers.
- Each year $200 billion is spent conforming to complex and convoluted income tax regulations.
- Inheritance taxes legally confiscate as much as 60 percent of the wealth accumulated over a lifetime of hard work.
- Local and state taxes have tripled in real dollars since 1960.
- We're paying billions in capital gains taxes on houses and investments that have actually lost money.
- Exorbitant taxes are forcing more and more people into the "underground" cash economy, growing twice as fast as the legitimate one.

If you're sick of getting beaten in the tax racket, you need to fight back by reading this book! It offers *real* solutions—including the end of the IRS!

THE TAX RACKET

Government Extortion from A to Z

Martin L. Gross

Ballantine Books • New York

Copyright © 1995 by Martin L. Gross

All rights reserved under International and Pan-American Copyright Conventions. Published in the United States by Ballantine Books, a division of Random House, Inc., New York, and simultaneously in Canada by Random House of Canada Limited, Toronto.

Library of Congress Catalog Card Number: 95-94414

ISBN: 0-345-38778-3

Manufactured in the United States of America
First Edition: June 1995
10 9 8 7 6 5 4 3 2 1

To my wife,
a loyal companion in the struggle for freedom.

CONTENTS

Acknowledgments

I would like to acknowledge the assistance of several organizations that helped provide research sources and, in many cases, inspiration as well. They include the Citizens for an Alternative Tax System (CATS), the Tax Foundation, the National Taxpayer's Union, the Small Business Survival Committee, the Cato Institute, Americans for Tax Reform, the Citizens Against Government Waste, the American Legislative Exchange Council (ALEC), Citizens for a Sound Economy, the Competitive Enterprise Institute, the National Center for Policy Analysis, the Institute for Research on the Economics of Taxation (IRET), and the National Federation of Independent Business.

Others include the Agency for Inter-Governmental Affairs, the General Accounting Office, the Federal Communications Commission, the Securities and Exchange Commission, the Office of Management and Budget, the Bureau of Labor Statistics, the Census Bureau, the National Conference of State Legislatures, the Taxation Department of the State of New York, the National League of Cities, the National Association of Counties, the Securities Industry Association, the Department of the Treasury.

Several members of Congress and numerous public officials throughout the country, many of whom are as frustrated with high tax rates as we are, were also very helpful.

In particular, I would like to thank my editor and publisher, Matthew Shear, and assistant editor, Phebe Kirkham. Their talent and patience have been invaluable in making this project a reality.

"A wise and frugal government which shall restrain men from injuring one another, which shall leave them otherwise free to regulate their own pursuits of industry and improvement, and shall not take from the mouth of labor the bread it has earned—this is the sum of good government."

—Thomas Jefferson

THE TAX RACKET

Reform the System, Close the IRS, and Save America

"Nothing in this world can be said to be certain except DEATH AND TAXES," Ben Franklin wrote to a friend in 1789.

Were Franklin to return to America today, he would surely change the ancient saw to read "TAXES ARE DEATH," especially for a civilization such as the U.S. of A.

The nation is just waking up from twenty-five years of sleepwalking. We had watched mute as America became an endangered society, threatened not by pollution but by excessive taxes at all levels, from a dogged IRS to an insatiable Town Hall.

Just a few years ago, the antitax crowd was dis-

1

missed as "crackpots." American politicians taxed and
spent with a promise of Nirvana tomorrow as long as we
handed over our wallets today.

Well, tomorrow has arrived, and it turns out that our
bloated, wastrel governments at all levels are the true
"crackpots," apparently determined to weaken the economy and destroy our independence.

In fact, the beleaguered American family has involuntarily broken the symbolic four-minute mile of politics.
According to the Tax Foundation, they now pay an average of 40 percent of their income to Uncle Sam and his
hungry assistants in the states and localities. Taxes now
take more money from them than housing, food, and
medical care combined!

*At the same time, the federal income tax bite has
gone up some tenfold in real dollars since the Fabulous
Fifties.*

The cost of all governments—federal, state, and
local—has ballooned to 40 cents of every dollar earned in
the nation from Brooklyn to Burbank, a sinful mathemat-
ical equation and almost double the 22 cents we spent
under Harry Truman in 1950.

Today, our Tax Freedom Day—when we stop work-
ing for governments and put the first bite of tax-free food
in our mouths—is May 6 nationally. Bad enough, but in
New York it extends to May 24, some 144 days into the
year. Connecticut pays until May 22, followed not far behind by Minnesota, New Jersey, and California.

Spending Freedom Day, when all governments stop
spending our money, including borrowed funds, is now

May 18 nationally, and June 9, almost half the year, in New York.

The sad truth is that including deficit financing, we Americans now pay $2.6 *trillion* in some thirty-five different taxes to a cornucopia of governments and agencies, each with a lien on our pocketbooks. (In the back, a chart will help you figure out just how much the *taxmeisters* have dunned you for this year.)

That $2.6 trillion represents some $40,000 for each family of four, a fortune taken out of our mouths by our governments for supposed services which most Americans never see, and didn't want in the first place.

Our politicians now say they understand—that the revolution I asked for in *A Call for Revolution* in 1993 has taken place, and that their eyes have been opened.

Not really. President Clinton, in his hyperbolic "Middle Class Bill of Rights" (Harry Truman is turning over) is promising a $500 tax credit for each child in families earning up to $75,000.

A little help, but very little. What if you are a two-paycheck family making $76,000, and are hard-pressed to pay your exorbitant FICA, federal and state income levies, and constantly rising property taxes in high-priced suburbs? Don't you also deserve tax relief for your children?

And what happens if you earn considerably less, as most do, and have no dependent children?

In this new sociopolitical game, taxes are becoming chips in a class warfare rapidly engulfing America. Not only is the government picking your pocketbook, but it's also looking into it to see if you're eligible for tax breaks, student loans, or any of the "means tested" goodies offered by Washington.

You don't have to make $75,000, or even half of it, to be hard-pressed tax-wise.

Typical Household

You may be the average Joe and Jane, heads of the typical American household which takes in only $33,000 a year, $53,000 in two-paycheck homes. In that category, you'd think you're escaping the high dudgeon of the wealthier. Think again. Your taxes are staggering as well.

What is your *real* federal tax bracket? Fifteen or 20 percent? Hardly. It's 7.65 percent for FICA from the first dollar earned, and a 28 percent income tax on top for all monies over $39,000—an incredible marginal rate of almost 36 percent. And what about the strained self-employed person who pays almost double Social Security taxes? Well, read on.

High for a working person? One would think so.

When added to state income and local property taxes, it becomes a litany of *agita* for millions of Americans. High taxes makes anxious victims of us all, and in that, the nation is united.

The new Republican majority in the 104th Congress offers a somewhat better deal than the president. But like the Democrats, none of their schemes—except symbolically—faces the true reality. Whatever little is saved at the federal IRS level will be immediately eaten by the yearly automatic increase in FICA taxes (up to an income of $61,200 in 1995) and the constant rises in local property levies. One tax goes down a little, maybe. Two go up, definitely.

Be warned: The tax debacle is so entrenched that no first aid for taxpayers over the next few years is going to change the basic, punishing equation.

Washington is not the only operator of the tax racket. Since 1960, the cost of state and local government has risen 350 percent in real dollars and has now passed the *trillion*-dollar mark, the sign of bloated local bureaucracies.

Property taxes in many suburban communities—escalating with the cost of K-12 education—are a governmental water torture. Small homes in the New York tri-state metropolitan area which cost $200,000 have property tax bills of $5,000 and $6,000, beyond the ability of many to pay. And larger homes ($500,000 is not untypical in Westchester County, New York) have property tax tags that reach $12,000 a year and more.

Affluent Greenwich, Connecticut, for one, received an average 28 percent hike in residential taxes on July 1, 1994.

What's the basic problem? It is that we Americans can no longer afford our governments or the unwanted tithes that sustain them. And most don't know what to do about it. This volume will try to unravel that conundrum and come up with solutions, including some of dramatic proportions.

How widespread are taxes? Are there just the basic four or five to bedevil us?

Hardly. In the real world we are surrounded by them—oppressed by the heavy ones, needled by the typical, and annoyed by the minor. Collectively, they create a climate of oppression from which there's no escape and in which mental depression is a common side effect.

In researching this book, I have spotted over two hundred different taxes, and I'm only one person working with an ancient computer.

Tax Monster

Taxes are now extorted from most Americans through a multitude of levies. The hydra-headed tax monster includes, but is not limited to:

(1) FICA tax (Social Security and Medicare); (2) the regular IRS Income tax; (3) Extra Medicare taxes; (4) State Income tax; (5) School taxes; (6) Town or City Local Property tax; (7) County Property tax; (8) Personal Property tax; (9) Excise taxes on cigarettes, beer, whiskey, wine; (10) some sixty other Federal Excise taxes; (11) Local Sales taxes; (12) State Sales tax; (13) Inheritance taxes; (14) Use taxes; (15) Capital Gains taxes; (16) City Income tax; (17) Small Business taxes.

It continues:

(18) License taxes; (19) Gross Receipts tax; (20) Unincorporated Business tax; (21) Telephone taxes; (22) Cable taxes; (23) Gasoline taxes; (24) Hotel and Travel taxes; (25) Intangible Property, or Wealth, tax; (26) Car taxes; (27) Boat taxes; (28) Airline tax; (29) Double Dividend taxes; (30) Stock Transfer taxes; (31) Property Transfer taxes; (32) Parking taxes via meters and garages; (33) Environmental taxes; (34) Building and other Permit taxes; (35) Special District taxes; and (36) many other

hits ranging from Bridge to Highway taxes, euphemistically known as "tolls."

Is there no end? Absolutely not.

On Long Island, New York, they have "Swimming Pool" tax districts. Park districts proliferate everywhere. In one town in tax-happy Connecticut, a single street, Quail Road, is a tax district. Bloomington, Minnesota, home of the world's largest shopping mall, is now trying to recoup its money through a "Mall Tax" on hotel visitors.

Who can afford all these taxes? Very few of us.

The present federal tax bite alone can be dramatized in many equations, one of which is a self-employed person making $50,000 a year, who moves into the 41 percent federal FICA and income tax bracket at the regal sum of $39,000 taxable—not counting state or local levies. Believe it or not.

In New York City, an unmarried editor at a publishing house who thought she was "successful," finds she's paying $25,000 in taxes on a $60,000 salary. At some 42 percent, it's the perfect equation for personal fiscal disaster. (California has an even higher state income tax.)

At that level, it's not taxation. That's legal extortion, and thus the subtitle of this work.

The damage done by our tax system is not only to individuals but to the economy, which spirals downward with each new tax burden.

The best example is the New York tri-state metropolitan area, home of almost 20 million tax-oppressed Americans. New York City and its suburbs, lower Connecticut, and New Jersey are not only among the highest

taxed areas in the country but among the worst hit by the
last recession and the slowest to recover.

Mysterious Triangle
In this, the Bermuda Triangle of the tax racket, billions of
dollars, both federal and local, move mysteriously from
citizens' pockets into the vast official coffers.

Connecticut, which used to be a tax haven from
nearby New York, began its own state income tax in
1991. It has since lost about 100,000 jobs as firms and
people leave for kinder tax climes. Connecticut is one of
only two states to have lost population in the last census.

New York, of course, is the champion, working until
May 24 before citizens can put a bowl of tax-free chicken
soup on the table. In the last decade, New York has lost
40 percent of all the jobs that have disappeared in the
nation!

Residents of New York City need no lecture on
taxes. In addition to federal levies, there's a state income
tax that reaches 7.875 percent and a city income levy of
over 4 percent. If you're self-employed in the Big Apple,
you also have to contend with an Unincorporated Business Tax.

New Jersey follows close behind New York in its
late-in-the-year Tax Freedom Day. Governor Christine
Todd Whitman is cutting 30 percent of the state's income
tax, but that welcome move is mainly symbolic in that
high–property tax state.

Compare the sluggish growth of the Triangle with
the success of Florida and Texas, two states that have no
state income tax and generally low property taxes. They

lead the way. According to a University of Florida study, these two southern giants topped the nation in 1993–94 in job growth. Though only 10 percent of the population, they accounted for 20 percent of all new jobs created.

But why all this fuss about taxes now, just when America is in the midst of an economic boom?

What boom? Professional people, entertainers, stock brokers, and their ilk have had an economic field day. But the average American household income of $33,000 has gone *down* three years in a row, from 1992 through 1994. The wages of the average American worker, after inflation and taxes, have *decreased* 17 percent since 1973, the only Western industrial nation to so suffer. Some boom.

According to the World Bank, America's $24,750 per capita income is a third less than Switzerland's and $7,000 less than Japan's. And now we're in seventh place, beaten out by Sweden. Shame.

But we have a low 5-plus percent unemployment rate. No?

No. That mythical Washington figure appears that low because the government counts only what it wants to count. It doesn't, for instance, count nonworking adults on welfare, and their hangers-on partners, as being "unemployed." It falsely counts millions of part-timers and "temps" as fully employed. It doesn't count laid-off white-collar workers scrounging out a meager income as self-employed. Nor does it include as "unemployed" the long-term out-of-work who no longer draw benefits—and so are totally out of the government's fake statistical loop!

What's the real undoctored number of the un-employed?

According to a candid economist at the Bureau of Labor Statistics it's 15 percent, the very same figure estimated by Lester Thurow, noted MIT economist.

The suspicion that we're nowhere near full employment was confirmed recently when police had to handle a mob of people who had applied for *temporary* work at the GM plant in Tarrytown, New York.

So without a real boom, or full recovery, taxes matter more than ever. In fact, it's becoming obvious that America's high taxes are the major cause of our structurally weak economy, crippling any hope for a truly resurgent nation—unless we dramatically change our tax system.

Otherwise, the recoveries from each recession will be less and less vibrant, and the financial slope of our civilization will be one of continued long-range downdrift.

(One saving grace. The economic damage from taxes could spark a rebellion against the income tax—much like the 1994 election revolt against Washington's waste and overspending.)

Bi-Partisan Blame

Despite what partisans say, the tax horror we're experiencing is not just the work of one political party. After Democrat Truman and Republican Eisenhower—both of whom balanced the budget in an era of low taxes—*all* subsequent presidents of both parties trod the slippery path of deficit financing.

It began with JFK, and went through LBJ, Nixon,
Ford, Carter, Reagan, Bush, and Clinton. All have played
leading roles in increasing the size of an inefficient,
anti-intellectual, misshappen, often badly motivated
federal government. Thus began America's great slide
downward.

Those traits have overflowed into our states—forty-
three of whom have income taxes of up to 11 percent—
and to our profligate local governments as well.

The other villain is, of course, Congress, whose
excesses over the past years led to the "revolution" that
promises to cut Washington down to size. We'll have to
see if that work will be substantial or merely symbolic
"feel good" fiscal policy which will not solve our
tax woes.

The reality is that for the last quarter century, Congress and the presidents have betrayed us by concocting
tax laws that are insincere, unfair, and convoluted. We're
just learning that when it comes to taxes, Washington
speaks with an accomplished forked tongue.

Take the so-called 1986 Tax Reform Act. To great
fanfare, they passed what was heralded as a great boon to
taxpayers. Instead, vital money-saving deductions—
interest on most loans, sales taxes from states and localities, a strong IRA retirement plan, income averaging,
plus several other goodies—were taken from us. (By the
way, it also ruined the commercial real estate business.)

But politicians trumpeted that if we made that sacri-
fice, the top tax rates would come down to 28 percent.
Everyone would gain.

What has actually happened? It turned out to be a

Washington folderol. The deductions we loved are long since gone, but the higher rates have come back, with a vengeance. They have risen from 28 percent—slowly but inexorably during the Bush and Clinton administrations— back to 31, 32, 36, and 39.6 percent, just about where they were before.

All this, *plus* an extra Medicare tax, which no longer has an income ceiling, brings the marginal rate up to almost 42 percent. Meanwhile, the old deductions are gone.

(In any case, you should also know that the Medicare tax money no more goes to Medicare than it does to Iceland. In fact, none of the FICA tax is segregated out for Social Security but is deposited immediately in the general fund to pay for everything from the president's salary to cash for unwed mothers to subsidies for farmers. The simply fact is that FICA "contributions" are just a second income tax masquerading under a more acceptable name!)

So much for "tax reform."

Fooling the Middle Class
We've been fooled many times by a clever Uncle Sam, who specializes in tweaking the pocketbook of the middle class. For example, we now get only a rather puny $2,450 deduction on Form 1040 for each family member. But that amount should be double or triple just to keep up with inflation since the golden days of 1950.

That one trick has cost every family of four $11,800 in lost deductions a year!

Not only families, but the young are worried as well. They fear that their FICA "contributions" (a creative eu-

phemism for taxes) won't pay for both the Social Security of the aged today and their own retirement tomorrow.
In fact, a recent survey of twenty-somethings shows that
more of them believe in UFOs than think they'll ever get
a Social Security check.

They would be even angrier if they knew that Washington has stolen every nickel of the yearly FICA tax
surplus—some $400 billion from Social Security and
$130 billion from Medicare hospitalization insurance to
date. That money was supposed to have been put away
for them for the year 2015 and beyond, in cash. But now
it's all gone, squandered by the government and replaced
with meaningless federal IOUs that are part of a $4.9 tril-
lion national debt—which will never be paid back.

The aged have also become angry as the tax on their
benefits has skyrocketed. As a result of the 1993 Clinton
tax bill, supposedly "rich" aged couples with an income
of $44,000, or aged individuals with $34,000 income,
will pay taxes on 85 percent of their Social Security benefits. It's a cruel Washington joke on retirees hoping for
comfortable golden years.

Successful Americans who followed the dream, but
who are far from being rich, are angry as well. Two-
paycheck families with a combined income of, say,
$80,000 are shocked by their tax bills, making their "suc-
cess" hollow. With federal income taxes, two FICAs, expanded Medicare levies of over $61,200, state income
taxes and local property taxes, they're pushing up against
the dreaded 50 percent marginal tax bracket.

They've become special targets of the tax system.
The poor (except for the regressive FICA tax) are virtu-

ally free of income taxes. The bottom 30 percent of earn-
ers pay only 2 percent of the federal receipts. The middle
class, because of their numbers, pay the bulk of the taxes.

The tax system that penalizes someone who makes
$80,000 is called "progressive." By placing a fierce pen-
alty on success with higher rates as one earns more—
compounding the tax—it might better be called
"punitive." These citizens are paying much more than
their "fair share," a meaningless phrase now in currency
among glib tax-happy politicians.

No one has properly explained why such minor
"success"— the great goddess of our culture—should be
so denigrated and punished. When that happens, and the
great myths of our civilization become hollow, watch out.

Under the tax onslaught, some of us have become so
paranoid that we've come to believe that our politicians
are out to destroy us. Nothing could be further from the
truth. They want us sufficiently alive, like the Jews building the Pharaoh's pyramids—strapped to the oxen of time
and penury—so that we can keep working to pay our
taxes.

Excessive Burden
The sad part of the whole thing is that the current tax
burden is unnecessary. If Harry Truman's debt-free budget, on which we paid for the enormous expenses of the
Korean War, the Marshall Plan, and the GI Bill (the last
piece of social legislation for middle America) had just
gone up with inflation, the cost of Washington would today be only $800 billion, not the current $1.6 trillion.
We'd have no deficit and a 60 percent tax cut.

So, where does all the present multitrillion-dollar tax bite go?

To the largest collection of governments—85,000 in all, federal, state, and local—in the history of the civilized world. That's where. We're being hit from every direction. Each bloated jurisdiction pulls at us, insisting that their need for cash has greater priority on our pocketbooks than our own bills.

(Forget about saving money. Because of tax burdens, Americans have a skimpy 3.9 percent savings rate, about one-fourth Japan's, and a major cause of our high interest rates.)

Another reason for high taxes is that Washington has turned our states into colonies, agents for administering expensive federal programs which they must help support—often against their will. The states have had to increase taxes enormously to pay up to 50 percent of the enormous Medicare and AFDC welfare bill. Yet these are only two of eighty-one welfare programs *whose fiscal 1995 tab is $384 billion, more than a fourth of which has to be paid by the states.*

States have had to raise another $100 billion in taxes to pay for Washington-dictated unfunded mandates such as Motor Voter; law enforcement and prisons; clean air and other environmental projects; Americans with Disabilities, or whatever programs our Beltway masters divine, but for which they have no intention of laying out a nickel.

This expensive federal coercion is, of course, a blatant violation of the Tenth Amendment to the Constitution, which protected the states against such forced federal spending. It says, in full:

"The powers not delegated to the United States in the Constitution, nor prohibited by it to the States, are reserved for the States respectively, or to the people."

Today, it's a near-discarded piece of paper, ignored by Congress and by the cowardly Supreme Court.

(The House has passed a supposed antiunfunded mandate bill, but it doesn't cover mandates under $50 million, and only slows down, but doesn't fully prohibit, unfunded Washington pressures on the states.)

Another stimulus for high taxes has been the army of federal, state, and local government employees, some 19.2 million strong, few of whom die of overwork. For the first time in our history, we have more of them in government than in manufacturing (18.2 million), a sure equation for national disaster.

The cost of government employees is astronomical. Each federal civilian employee costs us $80,000 in cash for salary, benefits, and pension, *plus a collective half-trillion dollars* in unfunded pensions.

A study by the American Legislative Exchange Council shows that privileged government workers at all levels not only earn more than private employees, but cost us $300 billion a year in extra pensions, an amount larger than the entire federal deficit.

The 1994 congressional elections showed that Americans are dissatisfied with high taxes, but they continue to take it in the pocketbook.

Why?

One reason is that like the onetime secret of massive

government waste, which I helped expose in the *Government Racket: Washington Waste From A to Z*, we don't know the truth about our madcap tax system. From the IRS to the Town Hall, facts are purposely kept from us by our politicians and bureaucrats, to whom taxes are their cherished "bottom line."

That's the purpose of this book, to explain—in forty chapters arranged from A to Z—the full extent of the taxes we pay plus subterfuges, lies, irrationalities, stupidity, and self-destructiveness of our present tax system, nationally and locally.

Simultaneously, I will outline ways to drastically change the income tax structure so that we can again flourish as a wealthy nation, much as we did thirty years ago.

The Quick and The Poor

And whatever our income, we aren't always quick or solvent enough for our tax masters, who insist on their pound of cash on time and in full. To get it, they're empowered with such tools of persuasion as interest, exorbitant penalties, even seizure of our material goods—even our homes.

Last year, the IRS, which has 110,000 employees and a $10 billion budget, made 10,000 seizures of taxpayer properties, issued penalties in the $23 billion range, and was the perpetrator of many horror stories, including the heart-wrenching suicides of taxpayers, as we shall see.

(One recent action of the IRS defies description. They actually sent a tax bill for $6.4 million to the rela-

tive of a Pan-Am bomb victim, even though he hadn't received a penny in settlement!)

One reason IRS abuses have gone unchecked is that
many congressmen are deathly afraid of the agency, fearful they will become the target of audits, hounding, or
worse.

One man who's not cowed is Senator David Pryor,
Democrat of Arkansas and courageous author of the Taxpayer Bill of Rights.

Says Pryor about the IRS: "When we held hearings,
a parade of witnesses provided numerous examples of
honest taxpayers whose lives were chewed up by a relent-
less bureaucracy. . . . In recent years a startling pattern of
IRS abuse and overzealousness has emerged from coast
to coast."

Pryor, who is convinced the IRS has not really reformed, is now seeking congressional support for a stronger Taxpayer Bill of Rights II. He offers tale after tale of
innocent harassed people whose lives were maimed by
the IRS.

A divorced woman struggling to support her three
children by working as a $4.50-an-hour cook in a Phoe-
nix restaurant was anxiously awaiting her $614 income
tax refund. Instead she got a notice from the IRS that
they were confiscating that money toward the unpaid
taxes of her ex-husband, some five years after their
divorce!

Soon after, she was hit with $3,666 in taxes and in-
terest and penalties on her ex-husband's account. Franti-
cally, she sought help from the IRS as a legal "hardship"
case, but they turned her down. Fortunately, a local tax

attorney found that the IRS had slipped up on a technicality and saved the woman from total ruin.

"Acting as both judge and jury," says Senator Pryor, "the IRS has used its sweeping authority to confiscate income or property of thousands of single mothers to pay the debts of their ex-husbands."

The Internal Revenue Service has replaced the Soviet Union in the affections of many Americans. But we should also remember that the IRS is the Frankenstein monster of the United States Congress and our presidents, who have created the imperious Tax Code the IRS often unfairly and inaccurately enforces in the first place.

This book will not be a catalogue of IRS victims and gremlins, *although we will show the convoluted nature of the tax codes and demonstrate, through fact and anecdote, the agency's excessive—probably unconstitutional— power over taxpayers.*

But in general I will do what I do best, which is to explain and analyze the tax world in detail, then offer reforms so that citizens can make the tax revolution America so desperately needs.

The centerpiece of the tax racket is the irrational Internal Revenue system, which must be indicted for its many failings. Here then is a Bill of Indictment that must be prosecuted if we are to survive as a healthy nation.

The present Internal Revenue system:

1. Forces Americans to become nervous, compulsive bookkeepers for the government.
2. Discourages savings and investments.
3. Abuses honest citizens who have tax problems.

4. Is overly complex and arcane in its tax codes.
5. Seizes property and bank accounts without due process.
6. Takes too much money out of the economy.
7. Requires confession of personal finances and destroys privacy.
8. Levies excessive interest and penalties.
9. Is error-prone in its advice and notices.
10. Violates our basic civil rights.
11. Encourages evasion through high marginal rates.
12. Changes its rates and rules too often.
13. Makes it necessary for many taxpayers to use costly professional help.
14. Keeps cutting back on taxpayer deductions.
15. Punishes success with a vengeance.
16. Creates fear, anxiety, and confusion in the population.
17. Makes arbitrary decisions against taxpayers.
18. Probably operates unconstitutionally.

Subterranean Economy

One obvious symptom of its failure is the phenomenal growth of the untaxed Underground Economy, run by people who believe they can only stay solvent by cheating the IRS.

"Your bill is $65," says a plumber in a mild whisper. "But if you pay me in cash, it's only $50." They even accept checks made out simply to "CASH."

How large is this trend?

It's more than a trend among service people. It's an

epidemic. The Underground Cash Machine is growing 8 percent per year, more than double that of the Above-ground one that pays taxes. It will cost the Treasury an estimated $150 billion this year.

To that, add another $200 billion—the cost of preparing the ridiculously complex IRS returns, both in lost taxpayer time and the fees of accountants who massage the numbers for Internal Revenue. Just the three volumes of IRS *forms* alone take up over five thousand pages!

So what, skeptics might say. Haven't we always been burdened by income taxes in modern times? Is the fuss only false nostalgia?

Actually, no. Things really were much better in America in the 1950s and 1960s.

Our memories of tax bliss after World War II are quite true. Even before that few paid any income taxes. On the eve of Pearl Harbor only one in seven Americans were even required to file returns.

That changed with World War II, when the Ruml Plan—paying your taxes as you go (or went)—came into effect. It was continued after the war because the government liked getting your tax money as you earned it. Better accruing interest in their bank than yours.

Then in the postwar years, we entered a period of financial, and tax, heaven.

Was it really that good? No, for most people it was even better.

Let's go back to 1950, the great old days under Harry Truman, and look at Mr. and Mrs. America, a couple called the Stephens, and their two children.

Jack Stephens made $3,300, the average national

income. In the fashion of the day, his wife did not work, and more important, didn't have to. They lived in a three-bedroom ranch house that had cost $10,000, and on which they paid $207 in property taxes. The thirty-year, 4 percent mortgage payments were $55 a month.

But what about his federal income tax?

It was virtually nonexistent. Each family member had a $600 IRS personal tax exemption, which totaled $2,400. Then, Stephens had deductions of $300 in mortgage interest, plus the property tax exemption, $70 for sales taxes, and $95 for the interest on car and other loans.

(Both latter deductions have been taken from us by the well-paid, if indifferent, Congress of the American people.)

Total deductions for the Stephenses for 1950: $3,072. Taxable amount $228. The income tax rate at the time was 20 percent. *Therefore Stephens owed Uncle Sam all of $46 that year.* Added to that was $9 in New York State Income Tax. The total income hit was $55, or less than 2 percent of their earnings. (The national average for federal income tax was then 2 percent!)

The FICA tax was 1.5 percent up to $3,000, or another $45. The total federal and state tax bite was $100 out of $3,300, or just over 3 percent. Believe It or Not.

Next door lived the Gordons, a more prosperous family with a $5,000 income. Their property taxes were the same $207, and their deductions approximately the same.

What did they pay in federal taxes? Easy. Twenty percent of $1,900 taxable after deductions, or $380, less than 8 percent of their income. Their FICA tax was also $45, and the state income tax was $40. The total was $465, some 9 percent of their $5,000.

Frightening Update

And today? You don't want to know.

Both couples lived in the Town of Oyster Bay on Long Island. The Stephens' house is now occupied by their son. (The older folks moved to Florida.) The new property tax? It has gone up 2,600 percent and is now $5,700!

Young Stephens's income is now $43,000. And his taxes?

His FICA tax is $3,300. His federal income tax is $4,000, and his state taxes are some $1,000, or a subtotal of $8,300. To that add $1,000 in sales and excise taxes (nondeductible), or $9,300—22 percent of his income.

But that's not all. To that we must add his $5,700 property tax, making a total of $15,000 in taxes, 35 percent of his income and several hundred percent more than his father paid. (He actually pays a smaller percentage of his income than most New York State residents.)

The Gordon house is now occupied by the Masons. They are in the same economic class as the prior owners, and the $5,000 income is now a two-paycheck income of $65,000. Mr. Mason is a marketing executive, and his wife works as a real estate saleswoman. Their tax bill? The property tax is also $5,700, and their FICA tax, which now goes up to $61,200 of gross income, is $4,682. (Plus $55 extra Medicare tax because they earned more than the maximum.)

The Masons' state income tax is $2,000, and the federal income tax for him, his wife, and one child is $9,500. Their sales and excise taxes are $1,000, for a total of $22,700! It's money they cannot afford, especially if they ever expect to send their young son to college.

Of course, America didn't invent punitive, destructive taxes. The tax con has been part of world history for thousands of years, and generally operates with the same rhythm. First, it permits the nation, or area, to grow rapidly and strongly on low taxes—as once happened in America. We now see that phenomenal growth, accompanied by low taxes, in the Pacific Rim, from Hong Kong to Singapore.

Once affluence is achieved, history shows us that the *taxmeisters* raise the ante, and put in expensive governmental programs which they believe will reelect them, as it often does during prosperous periods of wealth building.

Meanwhile, the higher new taxes start to wreak financial havoc, after which the community goes into first a mild, then a severe, decline, finally ending in destruction. It is a pattern of world, national, regional, and local history, and we are seeing it take place before our eyes.

This cycle of building and destroying cultures through taxation is unending. As Charles Adams demonstrates in *For Good and Evil: The Impact of Taxes on the Course of Civilization*, taxes have destroyed one civilization after another, from Mesopotamia to Russia to the once-proud Bulldog of Britain. *All evidence shows that it is now working its clever ravages on Mr. and Mrs. America, circa 1995–96.*

Without sounding too chauvinistic, America had brilliantly avoided most of the folly of other nations—until the last thirty years. We escaped injury from the tax parasites, enabling us to create the world's greatest nation, with nary a runner-up.

We owe much of this former beneficence to the genius of James Madison, father of the Constitution. He predicted that if Americans were not vigilant, they would suffer the "oligarchy" of the federal government, which has made him our native Nostradamus.

But we have not been vigilant, and we no longer respect his wishes, to our grave detriment.

In the U.S. Constitution, Article 1, Section 9, Subsection 4, it simply states that there shall be "no capitation" or "direct" taxes, meaning no head or income tax.

That stroke of genius enabled America to grow phenomenally, unburdened by any real contact between the citizen and his government except in case of war. Meanwhile, countries around the world atrophied, burdened by taxation.

The income tax was temporarily put in by Lincoln during the Civil War, and in the 1890s, Congress tried to institute one, but the Supreme Court ruled against it based on Article 1, Section 9. Then, in 1913, under the guise of taxing only the rich robber barons (watch your pocketbook!), Congress pushed through the Sixteenth Amendment to the Constitution making the income tax legal, which was surely the gravest mistake in the history of our nation.

That amendment is a simple one-paragraph statement, hardly symbolic of all the damage it has wrought.

It reads, in full:

"The Congress shall have power to collect taxes on income, from whatever source derived, without apportionment among several States, and without regard to any census or enumeration."

Simply worded and simply devastating, as we have since learned.

Civil Rights Protection

One of the most significant aspects of the amendment is that it didn't detail how the tax was to be collected. Nor did it eliminate any of the civil rights protections granted to us in the Bill of Rights.

But they forgot to tell that to the Congress, or its creation, the IRS. That means that the methods now used by the Internal Revenue Service—despite what Congress has ordained in the Tax Code—cannot violate any other portion of the Constitution.

But with Congress's blessings, the IRS usurps the Constitution every day. It operates its levies on our bank accounts, its liens on and seizures of our properties totally against any precepts of the Constitution, or any rule of common law. The Bill of Rights is crystal clear as to what civil rights we have, and we can easily see how the Income tax system seeks to violate, then destroy them.

The Fourth Amendment of the Bill of Rights says it plainly:

"The right of the people to be secure in their persons, houses, papers, and effects, against unreasonable searches and seizures, shall not be violated, and no warrants shall issue, but upon probable cause, supported by

*Oath of affirmation, and particularly describing the place
to be searched, and the persons or things to be seized."*

The Fifth Amendment adds to our protection from
arbitrary and abusive acts from any government agency,
the IRS included. It states: *". . . Nor shall any person be
. . . deprived of life, liberty, or property, without due process of law. . . ."*

Obviously, the IRS is not acting constitutionally, a
pressing matter which we'll later discuss in detail (see
"Taxpayer's Rights").

When they conduct an audit, they *search* your papers without a warrant, claiming that it is "voluntary" on
the taxpayer's part.

When they place *penalties* on your taxes due, they
do it without a court order.

When they *levy* your bank account and take out your
money without your permission, they are making a seizure without a legal judgment against you.

When they *seize* your home because they say you
owe money, they are depriving you of property without
due process of the law. You've lost your constitutional
right to defend yourself in court.

When you contest the IRS in Tax Court, you are
guilty until you can prove yourself innocent, the opposite
of our whole system of jurisprudence.

How have they gotten away with it all these years?

One reason is the connivance of the Congress and
our presidents, and the cowardice of the Supreme Court
in enforcing the Constitution.

Negative System

Is there anything beneficial in our present method of taxation?

Nothing at all. It negatively affects many people psychologically. Taxpayers sense that their essential wealth is being drained from them. Perfectly innocent people feel as if they're living in the shadowland of crime when they make mistakes on their 1040s or give themselves the benefit of doubt on a sizable deduction.

A free people like ours becomes anxious at the mere mention of the IRS and their fearsome notices and powers, a reaction almost akin to what the Soviet people once felt about the KGB. In America, only the IRS has police state powers. No other governmental body can apply penalties and make seizures without the intervention of courts of law.

The IRS has turned Americans into a nation of nervous, compulsive bookkeepers, husbanding receipts, reading tax tip sheets and manuals, hiring expensive accountants, and working around the clock to ensure that they tell the full truth to the IRS, and still do not overpay.

We also tremble at the thought of our ignorance of the dark secrets in the eight volumes and 14,700 pages of the IRS code and regulations (Commerce Clearing House, Chicago, $93). New regulations are published daily in the Federal Register, and there are 200,000 pages of court decisions and interpretations of the unintelligible IRS code.

Apparently, we're expected to know and understand all this—ignorance being no excuse if you break the law.

But even CPA professionals can easily be tripped up

by IRS gobbledygook, codes written in arcane *incometaxese*, a language that can prove fiercely expensive for their clients.

Money magazine conducts a yearly "Tax Test" in which professional tax preparers fill out the taxes of a theoretical family. Forty-one accountants from New York to Honolulu handled a return whose true tax liability was $35,643. One preparer came out only $7 off, but thirty-five others figured the taxes much higher, most by several thousands. One accountant came up with an exalted tax bill of $75,450!

(The spread between the highest and lowest estimates by the "experts" was $44,000. Go figure.)

How can we free ourselves from this modern oppression?

If we're ever again to become an economically healthy nation, all income taxes—federal, state, and city—must be discontinued and replaced with a new approach, one which involves no figuring, confessing, or filing by citizens.

That requires closing down the IRS.

Stopping the federal income tax, surprisingly, does not require the repeal of the Sixteenth Amendment to the Constitution. That amendment only gave Congress the power to tax incomes, but it did not *require* it. All Congress needs is a simple majority to pass legislation eliminating the income tax. Once signed by the president, the IRS will be gone.

If we want to be sure another Congress or another president does not bring it back, then we must repeal the Sixteenth—a move that if properly worded will also

legally restrain states and cities from any longer decimat-
ing your paycheck.

Are the people angry enough at the income tax and
the political *taxmeisters* to back such an idea?

They still need more knowledge and consciousness-
raising, but I can personally testify that an antitax movement is alive and active in the grass roots—from
Montana to Mississippi and from Delaware to California.
It's all part of the same angry groundswell at waste in
government that ignited the congressional revolution of
1994 and awaits only leadership to move forward.

There is even a movement afoot in Congress. Majority Leader Dick Armey of Texas has introduced a "flat
tax," a system to replace the present "graduated" or "progressive" income tax. Armey's idea has some points of
merit and some deficiencies and we'll look at it more
closely (see "Flat Tax").

But flat or not, it's still an income tax, and not
the full reform we desperately need. Once and for all
we must say goodbye to the folly of the Sixteenth
Amendment, which has overwhelmed us.

The answer is to stop the income tax, at all governmental levels.

What will replace the IRS?

A national sales tax on all goods and services—
except housing, medical care, and food. The sales tax rate
will be a reasonable 13.5 percent, and as we'll show with
credible figures, it will take in enough money to replace
the individual income tax. If we also want to eliminate
the worker's share of the FICA, and deliver a full untaxed

paycheck, the total national sales tax would be 20 percent.

(See "How to Balance the Budget" with suggestions from my prior books, plus new information, all ready for the new era.)

This is a radical idea, but hardly a pipe dream. Congressman Bill Archer of Texas—the new chairman of the Ways and Means Committee who replaced Dan Rostenkowski—says he intends to introduce a constitutional amendment to do just that, to repeal the Income Tax Amendment of 1913. Such an amendment should be written so as to simultaneously ban income taxes in the states and localities.

Practical Idea

Why will a national sales tax work?

One reason is that it will be market-driven. If Congress raises the sales tax too high, consumption would be reduced and people and businesses would scream. Remember, no one has found a way to beat the wisdom of the marketplace or fully explain the irrationality of politicians.

The present tax system, on the other hand, is entirely in the hands of politicians. With their present taxing power (whether this president or the next, or this Congress or the next ten) they can confiscate as much money as they want and suffer only the spectre of defeat, as happened to the young congresswoman from Main Line Philadelphia who cast the deciding vote in favor of President Clinton's 1993 tax hike.

But with the IRS gone and a national sales tax in

place, the citizen—as both voter and consumer—will reign supreme. The economy will vibrate positively, as will the financial markets. Investments and saving, which will be tax free, will soar. The long bond will plummet, and America will experience an affluence the likes of which we've never seen.

People will have full control of their money and will spend and tax themselves as they see fit.

And what of the poor? Can they afford a national sales tax? With exemptions for food, medical care, and housing, we'll show how they will actually come out ahead.

To make it all a reality, all we need is a groundswell of support from Americans—who will never again have to file a financial confession with anyone, or save receipts or keep records as if their life depended on it. Nor will anyone ever again challenge their privacy or their papers, or their right to succeed, or penalize or threaten them for not following the government's stern dictas.

Several national organizations, including Citizens for an Alternative Tax System (CATS), the National Taxpayers Union, and the Tax Foundation, are working on this vital issue. And that historic reform is, of course, a main goal of this volume.

But what of the state income taxes that will be invalidated by the complete constitutional change we envision? Don't they need the money? Not really. Seven states now do nicely without an income tax, and several others are cutting it back or considering eliminating it. What one state can do, others can imitate.

Shorn of the ignoble duty of answering to Washington, their state, or city about their finances, our citizens will flourish as never before, leading America not only to a new affluence but to true peace of mind.

To do our part, we'll move from A to Z, from Airline Taxes to Marriage Taxes to Zany Tax Stories, stripping away the scrim of deception and complexity that covers our tax system. And with it, we'll wipe away the threat of punishment that has controlled us for generations, helping to set up the signposts of a citizens' tax revolution that will save America.

When that day comes, like the greatest Fourth of July, we'll all join in as joyous a celebration—replete with bonfires, church bells, and fireworks—as the nation has ever seen. Free at last!

And now, on to the alphabetical barricades.

1

AIRLINE AND AIRPORT TAXES

The Big Trust Fund in the Sky

When you call American Airlines and ask how much it costs for a round-trip ticket from New York to Los Angeles—without staying over a Saturday night—they'll quote you a price of $710, give or take a few dollars.

Of course, the airline agent adds, there's a $3 fee for the airport, which sounds reasonable enough.

What the agent doesn't tell you is that the real price of the ticket is considerably less—actually $646.

Why the difference of $64? That's because there's a 10 percent federal tax on all domestic airline flights, something the airline won't reveal unless you specifically ask. But of course, you wouldn't know to ask unless you studied the fine print on your last airline ticket. (With the airport fee, the tax is therefore $67.)

In fact, airline tickets are possibly the only item sold in the United States where the tax is *included* in the price.

Why? Obviously because the federal government, which is levying the tax, is one of the sneakiest operations in the nation. No private industry would dare pull such a trick. If they tried, they'd be under quick investigation by the Federal Trade Commission.

What about tickets for international travel?

Before you leave JFK or Miami International for a trip abroad, you have to pay a $6 Departure Tax.

Is that all? Hardly. For international plane travel, Washington has put in a whole series of "fees," the newest government euphemism for "taxes." There's a Customs Fee of $6.50, an Immigration Fee (you don't have to be an immigrant to pay it) of $6, a $1.45 Agriculture Fee (you don't have to be a farmer), and a $3 to $12 round-trip Passenger Facility Charge, depending on the airport.

Are these federal airline taxes deductible from your income tax?

No way. Many state and city taxes are deducted from your Form 1040, but not federal taxes. That means that you're a victim of double taxation. Of any given $1,000 income, for example, you might pay $300 to Washington. Now, you're paying another $64, and you can't deduct it.

Is that fair? Of course not. But no one ever claimed that when it came to taxes Uncle Sam was a model of either judiciousness or morality. By placing a tax on already-taxed money, Washington is breaking a social contract with its people, something which apparently doesn't phase the government.

But why such a large federal tax (10 percent) on domestic flights—higher than any sales tax in the country—and why so many fees on international travel?

It's all for the airports, responds the Federal Aviation Administration, part of the Department of Transportation (DOT), one of the newer cabinet agencies in Washington. (We now have fourteen, going on fifteen, while Harry Truman had only eight.) The answer, says the DOT, is that all the money goes into an Airport and Airways Trust Fund, which desperately needs the cash to help build and renovate airports.

That makes sense. The only trouble is that it's just not true.

Do they really need the money? In reality, the federal government pays less than 25 percent of the capital costs of airports, and the great majority of the money comes from local government and commercial sources.

But the government says "yes." They claim that the need is so great that in 1990 they had to raise the then 8 percent tax on domestic airline tickets to 10 percent.

Is it now enough? Or perhaps more than enough?

The answer is "much more than enough." So much money comes in—$5.2 billion last year—that the Airport and Airways Trust Fund has built up a giant surplus. In fact, they would have enough money to operate for two and a half years without raising another nickel!

In theory, the Trust Fund has $12.4 billion in the bank.

I say "in theory" because actually there isn't a red cent left, except as cash comes in each day from your tickets.

So where's all the money we've paid in airline tickets?

Sadly, it's mainly gone—swallowed up and spent by the General Fund of the federal government, and used to pay for welfare, government employees' health care, even the president's salary. The $12.4 billion surplus has magically been transformed into government IOU's, which are part of the $4.9 trillion national debt.

By just sitting there in nonnegotiable federal bonds, the giant airport surplus money is not building any runways or anything else connected with air travel.

As we'll see, the Airport and Airways Fund is just one of many from which Uncle Sam has "borrowed" every penny and promises to pay it back—someday.

Meanwhile, if he wasn't using your $64 on a Los Angeles ticket for everything else in the Beltway, the airline tax could easily be cut in half.

But as you and I know, that won't happen. Let's be happy that they're not looking to raise the Trust Fund surplus to $20 billion, and increase the ticket tax once again—just when you're ready to go on vacation.

Or are they?

But most important, as you're flying across the country and peering down at the neat farmland below, it should give you a good feeling to know that your ticket tax is helping some millionaire farmer get his subsidy check from Uncle Sam.

2

AUDIT

Like a Midnight Knock on the Door

The taxpayer had an extra half-acre of land on his building lot and decided to contribute it to the local conservation group. He'd be helping the environment and getting a charitable deduction on his income tax, a sort of double pleasure.

The appraiser thought the land was worth about $20,000, but being a "conservative" (read "frightened") taxpayer, the owner told him to keep it down to $10,000 for his IRS return.

Not long after, the taxpayer received the figurative "knock on the door in the middle of the night." It was the dreaded letter, a notice from the IRS that his taxes were being audited.

FEAR, FEAR, FEAR overwhelmed him. Not because he had cheated on his return but because the IRS, the closest thing a free nation has to the KGB, was on his case. And he was no James Bond.

Did he have anything to worry about? All his income was from salary and the W-2 was sent in to Uncle Sam. So he expected little danger there. His land gift was pegged at below its true value, so if the IRS checked, there'd be no trouble there either. But what about all those hidden tax interpretations he knew nothing about? Just the general fear of the IRS, now ingrained in the American ethos, kept him awake nights worrying.

He told his accountant to handle the audit, willing to pay the extra fee to avoid the stress.

The morning of the audit, he got a call from his accountant at the IRS office.

"They object to your $10,000 deduction and suspect the land is not worth that much," his accountant told him on the phone.

"But it's worth twice that, as I told you. I just cut it in half to be conservative."

"Well, you made a mistake," he said.

"What do they want?" the taxpayer asked, his mind contemplating what job he could best get in a minimum-security federal prison.

"The auditing agent says if you cut the value of the land to $9,000, they'll settle."

"SETTLE! SETTLE!" the taxpayer shouted.

The moral of the story? The IRS has powers not granted to anyone else in America, even the president, and they're not beneath abusing them.

The taxpayer was afraid because he had heard how the IRS can put your life, psyche, and finances in a snarl if you tangle with them excessively. Besides, challenging the $1,000 in Tax Court would cost more in legal and accounting fees. The taxpayer signed the settlement paper.

The IRS, of course, had engaged in a legal shakedown. The auditor had no idea what the land was really worth, nor did he care. Nor did he investigate by calling the appraiser. He just wanted to collect some money any way he could. That's not the stated purpose of IRS audits, but it's apparently typical in the hands of overeager IRS agents trying to please their bosses.

The land gift case is quite benign when compared to some audits, which can be very tough and psychologically abusive, even when the IRS is patently wrong.

A house painter in Texas quickly learned that the other side holds all the cards in an audit. It seems the computer had spewed out a conflict, and the painter was called in to explain it. His Form 1040 showed that he had received some $14,000 from a general contractor for painting a house. But the contractor's Form 1099 showed that he had paid the painter $35,000.

The contractor could only document the $14,000 payment, claiming he paid the painter most of the $35,000 in cash. The painter denied it, swearing that the $14,000 was all he had received. Who was telling the truth?

As is IRS custom, the local office decided the painter was guilty until he could prove himself innocent. He had to show that he *didn't get the cash*. Not only was that impossible, but it was a backward version of our usual justice system. Having failed to prove that he didn't do something, the painter was billed $17,000 by the IRS, including penalties and interest.

An immigrant from Mexico with five children, he was frustrated. How could he oppose the powerful IRS? He'd have to sell his pickup truck and his small house to satisfy the debt.

Luckily, he had previously painted the house of a local tax attorney, who listened, then took the case without a fee. *When the attorney read the IRS file he was outraged. The IRS admitted that they didn't believe the contractor's story that he had paid the painter in cash.* But since the IRS had the painter in their collection clutches, they pressed their case.

The attorney filed suit in the U.S. Tax Court where, topsy-turvy, the painter was guilty unless he could prove himself innocent. The IRS won the case and the painter had to pay up.

The distraught painter borrowed $17,000 from his relatives and paid off the IRS. Meanwhile, his attorney was furious at the injustice. He personally borrowed $75,000 to continue the case in the U.S. Court of Appeals. This time, the verdict was different. The higher court overturned the Tax Court, stating that the IRS had acted in a "clearly arbitrary and erroneous" manner.

The IRS audit system—which last year brought in $5.7 billion from individuals in additional taxes, penalties, and interest—is a strange and alien world which confuses, frightens, and often abuses the most honest of taxpayers. It was supposedly designed to catch crooks, liars, cheats, thieves, and not to bedevil innocent taxpayers. Nor, says the IRS, is it supposed to be used to raise additional revenue, but only to collect any unreported or inaccurately reported taxes.

But, of course, that's simply transparent IRS propaganda, something they're expert at, as our charitable landowner learned. Though most taxpayers are not audited because the government believes they're cheating, 85 percent ended up coughing up new money to Uncle Sam. In 1993, the IRS audited a million Americans, who paid an average of some $2,500 in additional taxes and penalties (not counting back interest) in order to get out of the process—and often the auditing room—with their pocketbooks and nerves intact.

The IRS likes to think they're fair, and sometimes they are. *But when they're called on a mistake, they can be vengeful, especially if the whistleblower is one of their own.*

One veteran IRS agent learned that a taxpayer she was auditing had received a $500 assessment twice by mistake. When she mentioned it to her superiors, she was told to collect the money anyway. "If the taxpayer is stupid enough to sign for it, you assess it." She was also reminded that if the quota for closing cases wasn't met, the district director wouldn't get his merit-pay bonus, a common hustle within the IRS.

A good citizen, the agent went to the agency's internal affairs people and spilled all. But instead of corrective action against the others, *she was harassed by the agency.* "I was audited," she explained, and her coworkers were questioned about her personal life. Finally, when the job began to affect her health, she resigned.

It's obvious that when we're audited, we're entering a strange new world with no parallel in a free society. Naturally, we have to handle it with extreme care. The house painter was fortunate he had an attorney, but some people try to handle it themselves, which experts think is a *big* mistake.

"Taxpayers talk too much," says a former revenue agent. "It's always best to have someone represent you for a fee."

Three types of people are entitled to plead a taxpayer's case in an audit: attorneys, CPAs, and a lay category called "Enrolled Agents," either former veteran IRS staffers or self-educated types who have passed a stiff two-day IRS exam. If you're being checked by a "special agent," it could mean they suspect criminal activity. Then a lawyer is your best bet.

The audit system is something all taxpayers should be familiar with, just as self-protection. In a typical year, the IRS audits about 1 percent of the 114 million individual returns they receive. Sometimes the inquiry is minor, such as leaving out $26 of reported bank interest on your 1040. Those can usually be handled through the mail.

In most other cases, you'll be asked to come to an IRS facility for an "office audit." If the situation is complex, or it's a business, you may be scheduled for a "field audit," the field being your office or your home.

The typical auditing agent at the IRS office, say experts, is someone *not* schooled in accounting or law, but who has received auditing training.

In that never-never world where you leave most of your civil rights at the door, you have to tread lightly. In-your-face tactics with Big Fiscal Brother, say former agents, will not usually work.

Experts say not to get too friendly, or to try to impress the agent. Best to handle yourself as if you're a good witness in court. Don't bring up any subject the IRS is not covering. Often the audit is narrowly defined, and you may enlarge it with your big mouth. Every extra word could cost you.

Who gets audited? Former agents say there are several red flags that increase the normal one hundred to one odds.

They include: (1) people with a sudden sizable jump in income; (2) those with incomes of $100,000 or more; (3) self-employed people; (4) people with home offices who take in less than their deductions; (5) those who cash in a retirement plan and keep the funds rather than roll them over; (6) those who fail to document write-offs on business equipment; (7) people who put more into the self-employed retirement plans than they're supposed to, generally out of ignorance; (8) those with large charitable deductions; (9) people whose 1040 form doesn't jibe with their W-2s and 1099s in a major way.

A computer generally does the original checking, after which the returns are hand-examined to make the final choices.

Does the IRS single out people for special attention—because the president or the local IRS director has it in for them?

That used to be commonplace. Presidents regularly used audits as a political tool to shake up their enemies. President Kennedy reportedly set up the Ideological Organizations Audit Project to go after people he didn't like. Johnson and Nixon continued his program, adding newsmaking criminals and political opponents, especially antiwar protestors. The Watergate tapes revealed that Nixon even contemplated using the IRS to audit major contributors to Senator George McGovern's campaign.

Ostensibly, that's all been stopped by the Privacy Act of 1976, and by IRS confidentiality codiciles (Section 6103) which limits disclosure to House and Senate tax-writing committees.

But no one has to hate you, nor does an angry computer have to spit out your Form 1040 for you to be audited.

You can be one of those "lucky" victims of a program called TCMP, or Taxpayer Compliance Measurement Program, an incredible anti–civil rights activity run by the IRS. The reason you've been selected for that audit is that you're just a random taxpayer with no particular problems (until they called you), which makes you a perfect guinea pig for the IRS.

What they're trying to find out is how best to audit others by auditing you. Is that a light once-over? Think again. The TCMP makes a regular audit look like a five-minute interview. In fact, it's been called a "whole life" audit in which *they can even ask you to produce your birth certificate to prove that you are you*!

Not just a few items, but your entire 1040, or 1040s, is gone over line by line, in infinite detail, along with a probe of your personal finances. You have, my friend, been chosen to be one of their "research" tools, as the IRS calls it.

How can you protect yourself against this massive invasion of your rights, your privacy, your dignity, and even mental stability?

Right now you can't. The surprising thing is that the IRS, in its 1992 annual report, acknowledges that they've been bad boys, calling the TCMP an audit that's "burdensome to the taxpayer." They even hinted they might do away with this intrusive probe. But not only is the IRS continuing the program, it's *expanding it* enormously!

The last TCMP, a relatively small one, was five years ago. The new one is scheduled for October 1995, when 153,000 returns, including individuals, Sub-Chapter S Corporations, partnerships, etc., will be scrutinized to the Nth degree, down to their fiscal underwear.

Regular audits are being expanded as well. Congress has given the IRS an additional $405 million to go full throttle after taxpayers in 1995. Instead of one in a hundred being audited, the chances will probably double. In the higher income brackets, chances will be even greater, perhaps as high as one in ten. Best of luck!

The government and the public often disagree on taxes, deductions, audits, penalties, and rights, and the two are in a constant battle (see "Taxpayer's Rights"). But so far, unless you're willing to give your sanity and pocketbook to win that fight, the IRS generally comes out ahead.

But please, if you're audited, under no circumstances get angry. It'll only cost you aggravation and money.

Instead, get even.

How? By using your voice to push Congress to eliminate not just audits, and their denigrating TCMPs, but the entire IRS.

3

BRIDGE TOLLS— OR TAXES

Hope You Can Swim

High on the list of the world's greatest lies (rivaling "the check is in the mail") is the promise that bridge tolls will be collected only "until the bridge is paid for."

New York's Triborough Bridge, built in 1936, cost only $83 million, all expansions included. Today, its tolls could pay for the whole thing in a matter of months. But do they still collect your cash?

Yes they do, and it's a healthy $6 round-trip, or some $1,000 a year for daily commuters, to boot.

They peddle a second tax lie as well. Once the bridge is paid for, they say they have to keep up the high tolls just to maintain the structure. That too belongs in the prevarication Hall of Fame.

What's the simple truth?

The reality is that many bridge tolls are among the most elegant schemes in the tax racket. They have virtually nothing to do with the bridge, which is just a front for a tax on travel—collected where they have you by the exhaust pipe, right in the middle of nowhere, much like the highwaymen of old.

Legend falsely has it that toll bridges operate at a loss. The truth is that many generate a giant surplus, often twice or three times the toll extracted from their captive car victims. Many bridge tolls are just a general municipal tax masquerading under another name. (Read "tax" for "toll.")

The Triborough Bridge and Tunnel Authority (TBTA) in New York, a true Goliath, runs an enormous tax trap throughout metropolitan New York. If you want to travel efficiently to the New York airports, for instance, you usually go over its main bridge, the Triborough.

Of course, you can use the Whitestone or the Throgs Neck Bridge, but they're part of the same conglomerate, and their tolls are the same. No escape there.

There is a free, nontax route through the streets of Queens, but it creates a problem. You might have to start out the day before to make your plane.

In addition to the bridge and tunnel business, the TBTA runs the Queens Midtown and Brooklyn-Battery tunnels, as well as other businesses it has no business being into. They own the white-elephant New York Coliseum and even the corruption-ridden Jacob Javits

Convention Center—all supported by your bridge tolls. Excuse me: *bridge taxes.*

How much of a profit do these modern highwaymen take in?

As much as $10 million? Please. The TBTA annual report shows that their surplus went up from $238,333,000 (almost a quarter of a billion) in 1992 to $337,138,000 the following year.

Meanwhile they cried poverty, and on January 1993 raised the tolls by up to 50 percent, to the disgust of car owners.

Where does this ill-gotten money go? To the bridges?

No way. All of it is diverted to support other governmental functions. Every time you use a New York toll bridge, you're paying for the city's subways and buses, which you probably never use. The bridge profits go to the New York Transit Authority and even help support train commuters in Connecticut!

It's a wonderful combination of extortion and welfare, the reigning theme of much of American government.

Another bridge-tax conglomerate masquerading as a "toll" operation is the Port Authority of New York and New Jersey, which runs two tunnels, the two major airports, and four bridges including its star, the cash cow George Washington Bridge.

The GW is unique because if you want to cross the Hudson River by car from New York City, it's the only bridge. If you have to go to work or home between the

two states by car, it'll cost you $4 ransom each time.
(The tunnels cost the same.) The George Washington is
also the major truck route from Maine to Florida.

There's no free bridge or ferry across the Hudson,
which separates New York from New Jersey. That's not
only not nice, but is probably unconstitutional—
prohibiting free interstate travel without paying a tax.
(Remember the old Articles of Confederation and tariff
tax walls between the states?)

Is the George Washington Bridge a losing proposition?

Funny. It produces a huge annual surplus of $147
million. Where does the money go? Naturally, to support
the money-losing Port Authority Bus Terminal and the
PATH train from New York to New Jersey.

These tax plutocrats also operate a plush bureaucracy in the World Trade Center, which they
own—all with your money. The Port Authority's director makes $170,000 a year, more than the gover-
nors of the two states it joins. To be sure you know
how rich they are, they've spent $17 million of your
money on fancy art for their headquarters. So the next
time you shell out MONEY at the GW Bridge, think of
MONET.

Bridge toll-taxes are a national phenomenon, from
San Francisco to Philadelphia, some operating on their
own, others part of "authorities." There are about 125
significant toll bridges in the United States, according to
the International Association of Bridges, Tunnels and
Turnpikes, and round-trip tolls range from 50 cents to
$20 for the Chesapeake Bay Bridge and Tunnel.

What should we do about the bridge toll-tax racket?

1. State legislatures should prohibit the use of tolls for other purposes—like subways and trains.

2. Once the bridge is paid for, the toll-tax should be reduced drastically.

3. Surpluses should not be used to support other business operations.

4. State agencies should audit these bridge authorities, then reduce their excessive manpower, salaries, and overhead.

Drivers who've all along suspected that they were being ripped off at bridge toll gates are 100 percent correct.

But what to do until the day of real reform comes?

I suppose we could always learn to become really good swimmers.

4

CAPITAL GAINS TAX

You Lose; Washington Wins—All the Time

Have you ever had a capital gains tax coup where you made a profit, then paid less on your income tax than the regular rate?

Well, Mr. Babcock thought he had one—until he learned the brutal truth.

He lost his executive job in the insurance industry in Hartford, Connecticut, and decided to leave that high-cost, high-tax state and relocate in Florida with his wife. Not only was the weather better there, but Florida has no income tax.

Unfortunately, real estate was in a deep down market, and he had to sell his house cheaply. But fortunately, he had a small cushion in stocks. He had bought 1,000 shares of General Motors for only $25 a share at a low point in 1974. Now he was going to sell it for $50 a share for a supposed good profit of $25,000. (The peak price was $65, but he's not a hoggish investor.)

But he had one hurdle—Uncle Sam. Babcock had taken the risk, been patient, even nervous over the years as he sweated out each GM downturn. Now that he was cashing in he had an unsolicited partner in the IRS, waiting expectantly in the wings for the capital gains tax on the profit.

Did Babcock really make a profit? At first glance, it seems so. He paid $25,000 for the GM stock, then sold it twenty years later for $50,000. A simple $25,000 profit, no?

No. He actually lost money—lots of it, and twice.

What Uncle Sam conveniently forgets in figuring his 28 percent capital gains tax is that old devil inflation. Babcock's $25 per share purchase and $50 sale is like comparing apples and pomegranates.

The intelligent question is: How much did he pay for the stock in 1995 dollars? That is: What's the real dollar cost of his GM stock *after inflation*?

Simple. The Consumer Price Index has since gone up three-fold, which means that in current dollars, he actually paid $75 a share for his GM stock! So instead of making money, *Babcock actually lost $25 a share*. In real money, he dropped $25,000 on his investment. Just to break even, he would have had to sell it for $75 a share, about what he would have received had he just left the money in a savings account.

Oh, excuse me. Mr. Babcock was injured twice. He

lost $25,000 to inflation, and then had to pay the IRS a
capital gains tax of 28 percent, or $7,000. So all told,
Babcock lost $32,000 on his so-called capital gain.

But, we're regularly told not to fret, that lower capital gains taxes are just a gimmick for America's rich. Ordinary people supposedly have no use for tax bargains at
a 28 percent rate instead of a federal high of 39.6 percent
for ordinary income. (It can reach to 42 percent!) Right?

Wrong. The reality is quite the opposite. Every
American who owns a share of stock, a home, or a mutual fund, or a retirement fund, is eventually subject to a
capital gains tax. *In fact, government figures show that 55
percent of all capital gains taxpayers earn $50,000 or
less a year.* Fifty-one million Americans own stock, and
almost 60 percent own their own homes, property that's
bought and sold more often than once a decade.

So much for Mr. Goldfinger and the IRS.

Capital gains can be delayed on a home *if* you rein-
vest the full amount of the sale in another primary
residence—which eventually catches up with you. But
vacation homes bear the full brunt of the present capital
gains tax racket.

If a ski lodge, for example, was bought in 1975 for
$7,500 and sold today for $20,000, Uncle Sam would hit
you with a capital gains tax of $3,500 on the supposed
profit. *But it's all supposed.* In real dollars, you actually
lost money over the twenty years.

This Washington racket is called "no indexing," a
trick that helped break the middle class from 1948 to
1982, when income tax brackets were finally indexed for
inflation. But property values—whether houses or

stocks—were never indexed, a convenient "oversight" that's proven very expensive for taxpayers.

Another of Uncle Sam's fiscal sleights of hand is that he collects capital gains taxes when you win, but like Pilate, washes his hands of the affair when you lose.

That's what happened to thousands of investors in IBM. The once-charmed blue chip was $155 a share in 1985 and supposedly headed upward. Instead, by 1994, it hit a bottom of $43 a share, when many bailed out. Today, it's back in the 70s, but still only half its high.

Does Uncle Sam take care of those IBM losers when they file their income taxes?

No way. Greedy Sam charges 100 percent of your profits at a 28 percent rate, but lets you take only $3,000 a year in losses if you have no capital gains to balance it against. But don't worry. If you lose $100,000 in the market, you can write it off in only thirty-three years.

The middle class is the real victim of the present tax law. Among people with incomes below $100,000, the loss to inflation was greater than all their capital gains. Yet they paid the IRS through the veritable nose. They paid $5 billion in capital gains taxes, but actually *lost* $11 billion in real dollars.

But we need the money, say the tax writers in green eyeshades. That's why they increased the capital gains tax in the Tax Reform Act of 1986—from 20 to 28 percent.

The Congressional Budget Office was confident. They predicted that despite the higher tax, capital gains profits would rise to $269 billion by 1991.

How did the federal soothsayers do?

Naturally they proved to be dead wrong. The results were exactly the opposite, as economic law (not taught or followed in Congress) dictates. The capital gains income *dropped* dramatically, going down to $108 billion. The feds were off some 150 percent, enough to grant them an "F" in Economics 101.

No one, especially the government, gained anything. The Joint Economic Committee showed that the tax increase cut the capital gains profits in half in the following five years. TAX REVENUES FROM IT DROPPED 12 PERCENT. The *loss* to the government was $58 billion!

Why? Because people aren't stupid. They held on to their assets rather than sell them and pay the heavier tax.

The present law locks in capital everywhere, whether in stocks, homes, or businesses. (The amount has been estimated at $7 trillion.) Not only does that reduce revenues for Uncle Sam and the states, but it slows down the economy, with fewer jobs and lower wages for working people.

The hike in capital gains tax to 28 percent also slowed down the venture capital business—people with money backing people with ideas. After the 1986 tax hike, venture capital investments tumbled 70 percent.

What's the solution?

1. Index all property—tangible and otherwise—for inflation before figuring the capital gains tax.

2. Cut the tax itself down almost in half. This will move people out of old situations into new ones and stimulate business.

Lawrence Lindsey, a member of the Federal Reserve

Board, believes the ideal capital gains tax rate is 15 percent.

Why? Because not only will it stimulate buying and selling but would *maximize* federal revenue. Win-win!

3. Combine the two. The Institute for Policy Innovation says that the mix of indexing and a cut to 15 percent will do wonders: increase the GDP by $1.3 trillion over five years, create a million new jobs, boost annual wages by $1,500 (maybe take us out of seventh place worldwide), and *add* $211 billion in tax revenues.

4. Enact a ZERO CAPITAL GAINS TAX. That's the theory of Congressman David Drier of California, who heads a bipartisan caucus pushing the concept. This idea does lose revenue for the government, but Drier believes that by releasing trillions in tied-up capital, the economy will take off, bringing in more federal dollars and making up the loss.

The quickly developing countries in the Pacific Rim such as Malaysia and Singapore have zero capital gains taxes, which is probably why their economy is so robust.

Common sense tells us that the present system is folly.

It does no one—neither government nor taxpayers—any good. An intelligent Washington (an oxymoron?) should finally realize the truth.

Several efforts to reduce the capital gains tax are already under way in Congress. The major proposal would "index" property values and tax only half of capital gains at the person's own bracket. That would bring it down into the 14–20 percent range, lower than the pre-1986 level.

So before you sell any property, you might want to wait and watch. No sense giving greedy Sam even more than he wants.

And until the real tax revolution arrives and all capital gains are eliminated along with the IRS, the adage still goes:

"You lose; Washington wins—all the time."

5

COUNTY TAX RACKET

Who Needs It?

We Americans like to rail against our governments, but we still collect them like trophies—sometimes right around our necks.

There are 85,000 different governments in the nation including states, cities, towns, villages, boroughs, hamlets, and of course counties. In numbers there are 19,296 municipalities, 16,666 townships, and 33,131 special districts, all of them with their hands in our pocketbooks.

The county, a third layer stuck between the states and our local governments, is our most extensive, and expensive, operation.

Do we need counties, an iconoclast might ask? Most

citizens would probably be quick to answer. "Why, of course. We've always had them. How can we do without them?"

We must love them because there are 3,043 counties and they come close to bleeding us poor, taking $170 *billion* out of the economy with the help of 2.2 million county employees.

It's all paid for by the "county tax," which is sometimes hidden in the property tax bill. Other times it has its own line, broken out along with town tax, village tax, fire tax, police tax, water tax, and school tax. Usually, the county tariff is the second largest after the champion, the levy for schools (see "School Taxes").

Counties come in all sizes, from Loving County, Texas, population 107, to Los Angeles County, California, a giant with a population of almost 9 million and the largest nonstate government in the nation.

They also come in all shapes with no rhyme or reason except pure historical accident. Some are parts of cities, as in New York City, which has five counties within its borders—Kings, Queens, Bronx, Manhattan, and Richmond. Other counties are bigger than the city they encompass. Cook County, Illinois, covers the entire city of Chicago plus dozens of suburbs.

The super-monster Los Angeles County is three times as populous as the city whose name it shares. The "County," as it's simply known, includes not only the city of Los Angeles, but *eighty-eight other cities* including Beverly Hills, Pasadena, Long Beach, along with a million people in a screwball American invention called "unincorporated areas."

Suffolk, Nassau, and Westchester counties in suburban New York ($5 billion combined annual budget) are more grandiose and populous than most cities, and even several states. They include a giant package of cities, towns, villages, and hamlets, all wrapped up onto one map.

Westchester County, which sits atop New York City, has six cities—Rye, White Plains, Peekskill, Yonkers, Mount Vernon, and New Rochelle—plus fourteen townships and twenty-three villages, all with expensive overlapping governments which have driven property taxes through the roof. (No one knows, or will ever know, why smaller Rye is a "city" while larger Scarsdale is a "village.")

Nassau County on Long Island suffers from that same expensive epidemic of government. It includes two cities, three towns, and sixty-four incorporated villages, each with its own government. At the end of Long Island, Suffolk County has ten towns and thirty incorporated villages.

(Glory to the American politician and woe to the taxpayer.)

Duplication, overlap, and high taxes are the signposts of the COUNTY RACKET.

Take any governmental function in America and multiply it by three or four, and you have the story of monumental waste. Often, for example, three police forces—state, county, and local—will cover the same area.

The "county" idea is a carryover from the old country, England, where it enabled a local squire to maintain

control over a number of villages. It even served a purpose in nineteenth-century America, where it was the
glue for scattered village and farm areas.

But no more. Counties are now like cities with the
same overblown governmental problems and taxes, which
makes no sense at all.

Do we need them, as we asked before? Do we have
to spend $170 billion a year and support 2.2 million
employees?

Of course not. The whole thing is an anachronism in
modern society, a whole level of government we can
purge out of existence.

How do we know? Because one state, Connecticut,
with one swipe of the pen by former governor Abe
Ribicoff, wiped out all of that state's counties, which had
existed since colonial days! Today, instead of the counties, which went out of business in 1960, Connecticut is
cut up into 169 municipalities, each reporting directly to
the state.

There are no more middlemen and no more county
employees—except one part-time sheriff, an anomaly that
continues to this day. (Politicians seem to need some id-
iosyncratic nonsense.)

Everyone talks about wealthy "Fairfield County" in
Connecticut, the home of celebrities like Paul Newman
and George C. Scott and Kathy Lee Gifford, and the setting of so many society Hollywood movies. But Fairfield
County is now just a name on a map.

(One other state, Rhode Island, also has no counties,
a centuries-old secret no one ever talks about.)

What would happen if other states copied Connecticut?

Easy as pie. No matter the size of the state, it could be sensibly drawn up into geographically sound municipal areas, cutting out one layer of American government entirely and shifting county duties (which are often duplicated anyway) to them.

Conservatively, it would eliminate one million employees—let go by attrition over several years—and save us at least $50 billion a year.

It would also cut down one more tax that's strangling us.

Closing down the 3,043 counties will take political courage. But so will saving America from the tax monster.

Does Los Angeles County really have 9 million people? Why, that's more than in forty-four states of the Union!

6

DEDUCTIONS

Going, Going, Gone

There are three ways the *taxmeisters* squeeze American taxpayers:

1. Raise tax rates.
2. Tax something not taxed before.
3. Reduce or eliminate deductions.

The last item—cutting out deductions we once enjoyed—is the one politicians love the most. Raising tax rates usually starts a loud political hullabaloo and many politicians shy away. But deductions! They're relatively easy to sneak into law in committee without much public debate. They're in place before we wake up, if we ever do.

But remember, a lost deduction is the same as a tax increase.

The story of taxes on middle America has been one of constant *increases* in rates and *cuts* in deductions. As one goes up the other goes down and we suffer twice. In the last twenty years, the pendulum has been swinging against us with a deadening rhythm.

Take the prime deduction, the personal exemption we all receive on Form 1040 from the day of birth until we die. In the good old days of 1950, when the government was solvent and taxes were low, that was $600.

What should it be today—after inflation?

That could be figured several ways. If we use the Consumer Price Index, it would be almost seven times more, or $4,000 per person. Instead, if we measure it by the increase in the cost of houses and cars, today's personal deduction would be a more robust number.

In 1950, the average new car cost $2,210. And today? That price has just hit $20,000! That's a ratio of nine to one over 1950, which gives us an inflation-adjusted deduction of $5,400 per person.

Home prices have suffered even more. A typical existing home in 1950 cost $7,500. Today it's $106,000—about fourteen times as much, or twice the supposed rate of inflation. That means our $600 personal deduction on Form 1040 should now be $8,400!

Take a peek at your 1040 form. What is it today?

Exactly $2,450, a comic figure that allows the IRS to legally pick your pockets and keep you off balance at the same time.

What's the proper number? If we set a reasonable

nine to one—a compromise between the CPI and the cost of houses and cars—as the true inflation rise since 1950, the personal exemption should be $5,400, *more than twice the present figure.*

What does that mean for an average family of four? How big a hit have they taken in the pocketbook?

Just a loss of $11,800 in deductions a year, that's all. Often the difference between a painful and decent existence. No wonder the American family is tottering on the brink, courtesy of the IRS.

The deduction racket permeates the whole IRS code. Take sales taxes. We once had an automatic deduction figured from an IRS table. That's gone, a victim of the 1986 "reform" that wiped out all sales tax deductions. (That's made sales taxes a double-tax whammy, federal and state.)

A big loss was the sales tax deduction on a new car. Today, that typically means a loss of $1,200 in deductions. At the 28 percent bracket, that's like a federal tax increase of $336.

Every new tax law or "reform" passed by Congress seems to wipe out another deduction. Look at the supposedly innocent 1993 tax hike.

It's nickeling and dimeing us to death.

Do you have a small office in your home where you do extra work after hours? You've been deducting that for years. But no more. Now it must be your "principal" place of business if you want to take it off your taxes.

If you're self-employed, do you occasionally take someone out for a beer, or lunch? You used to be able to deduct it all, then it was cut to 80 percent. Now, courtesy of the 1993 tax bill, you can only take off half of it.

That 1993 bill had some mean teeth. Before, if you had to move for a new job, you could deduct the cost of scouting out a house, temporary living for thirty days, plus meals going to and from the new area. Now, you can only take the cost of moving your household goods and lodging on the way.

Want the definition of real chintzy? Before, you got the deduction if you moved thirty-five miles or more from your old place. Now it's got to be fifty miles, a fifteen-mile lost cause!

What an unconscionable hit? You used to deduct your costs of looking for a new job. *Now, you can do it only if the new job is in your old field.* If you're looking for something different, it's on you—tax-wise.

Charitable deductions are still in, but new rules are tightening the meaning of generosity. You can't deduct a pledge, and for any contribution of $250 or more, you need a written acknowledgment. Your cancelled check is not good enough anymore, though nobody knows why. And no more deducting $300 for all that cash you put into the plate at morning church service—unless the minister's willing to give you a *big* receipt.

There are other charitable deductions to watch out for. You can't deduct a donation of blood, or tuition paid to a nonprofit school. If you give your church property worth more than $500, you have to fill out Form 8283, otherwise the IRS will reject your generosity.

The once valuable medical deduction is disappearing. Once it was almost all deductible, then the threshold was raised to 5 percent of your income. After the 1986 "reform," the figure went up to 7.5 percent, meaning that a family with a $55,000 gross adjusted income can't take a nickel off until they've spent $4,125 in medical costs in one year!

Still another hit on the American family courtesy of Congress and its enforcer, the IRS.

Until 1991, cosmetic surgery was considered a legitimate medical deduction. No more. Nor can you deduct the cost of a maternity nurse for a healthy baby. But the courts have ruled that you can deduct the cost of a stop-smoking or a weight-reduction program if a doctor has prescribed it as "essential."

The famous 1986 tax bill also robbed us of deductions for interest on loans, including credit card interest and car loans.

A $15,000 four-year bank car loan at 12 percent costs the buyer $3,971 in interest. In the 28 percent bracket, that's a tax hike of $1,012. With the extra state taxes, it's grounds for despondency.

Even your itemized deductions are no longer safe if you're relatively successful. Once you reach a threshold income ($55,900 for a married person filing separately) you lose 3 percent of your deductions—from mortgage interest to property taxes.

That changed the 39.6 supposed top bracket to 40.79, to which you must add the 1.45 extra Medicare tax over $61,200. So now the *almost real max tax* is 42.44 percent, plus state income taxes—and going, going, going.

The *real* max?

Tag on 7.65 percent Social Security tax on the first $61,200, or some 13.2 percent more for the self-employed and you've hit the bad news 50 percent tax mark.

Had enough? Wait.

If you're in the upper income tier, you're no longer even considered a full person, exemption-wise. That measly $2,450 deduction gets cut step by step after you've passed an IRS income threshold. After that, you're worth less and less to yourself, tax-wise. Eventually your entire personal exemption is wiped out. Talk about self-esteem.

You used to be able to deduct most casualty or theft losses, but now it's almost impossible. The *taxmeisters* now require that you first take $100 off the loss. Then you can deduct the rest of it *only* if it's more than 10 percent of your gross income. If you had a $55,000 income, the loss would have to be almost $6,000 before you could deduct a penny.

Who are they kidding?

But there's a silver lining in this mad deduction world. You can't deduct your traveling expenses from your home to a first job, or from a second job to home. That's commuting. But in a spirit of munificence, the IRS will let you deduct the cost of travel from your first to your second job!

Of course, you wouldn't need a second job if we had a decent tax system.

Small perks that used to make the taxpayer feel good are disappearing as well.

Until the 1993 tax law, you could take your spouse along on a business trip—if they were valuable to the enterprise—and deduct their expenses. It was a nice touch of a once-considerate government.

- But no more. The meanie Congress showed their true colors in the 1993 bill. Now you pay the freight or you go alone.

What do we have to look forward to?

I'll let you in on a big secret. When Rostenkowski and Co. were debating the 1993 tax bill in the House Ways and Means Committee, two deductions were on the table for possible elimination. They were your mortgage interest and your local and state taxes.

They were saved only because of overwhelming anger and pressure from the public. That's one piece of luck, but mark me, they're not finished with us yet.

They'll just take away one more deduction after another on our Form 1040—until we get rid of the 1040 itself.

7

DIVIDEND TAXES

Two-Card Monte

Last year, millions of Americans received stock dividends on their investments. (Not everyone is on welfare, as the media sometimes makes out.)

That total was an incredible $80 billion—"B" as in "Perot"—and Uncle Sam smiled as he waited for his tax cut, some $30 billion.

What's so unusual? Afterall, dividends distributed to stockholders by corporations are personal income that has to be declared on Form 1,040. Don't they?

Yes, but this has a special twist. The dividends were already fully taxed by the time the investor received them. The corporation had paid a corporate income tax on the very same money, after which the investor had to

list it as personal income on his 1040—where it became
a choice double-tax morsel for the IRS.

*What Uncle Sam is pulling off is the world's greatest
tax racket, the double flimflam, the two-card Monte, the
envy of tax writers worldwide.*

Assume that a corporation pays a tax of 34 percent
on its profits. *After* that, they disperse dividends from the
remaining profit, or if not, out of retained earnings, which
have already been taxed as well.

With a typical 35 percent personal federal and state
income tax rate for many stockholders, and up to 48 percent for the top tier, we're talking about anything from a
net 57 percent to a 66 percent tax on the same money!
Now, that's not nice.

The double tax on dividends has nefarious conse-
quences for businesses as well. Corporations get IRS deductions for borrowing, so they go heavily into debt. On
the bottom line it costs them nothing. But since dividends
are not tax deductible, corporations are often stingy with
stockholder disbursements, short of killing their stock
price.

Even the Department of the Treasury isn't sure they
should be double taxing dividends. Kenneth W. Gideon,
the assistant secretary of the Treasury for tax policy
under President Bush, suggested changes but got nowhere. "This is an issue we're going to have to deal with
it in the 1990s," he stated.

No kidding. But thus far, under both Presidents Bush
and Clinton, there's been no action. The government is
still getting paid twice on the same money.

What's the solution to the vexing racket?

There are four possibilities for Congress:

1. Exclude stock dividends from personal income tax.

2. Don't tax corporations for any money paid out as dividends, just as the IRS now excuses them for their cost of borrowing.

3. Start a Comprehensive Business Income Tax plan in which corporations cannot deduct interest or dividends, but individuals wouldn't pay taxes when they receive them.

4. Tax-free pension funds and charities get their dividend checks taxed only once, at the corporate source. That's what should happen for all dividends, not just for a privileged few.

Is the tax-exempt relief from dividend double taxation significant to the rest of us? You bet your life. They own 37 percent of all corporate equities, which puts an unfair burden on others who get a few dollars in stock dividends—not to mention the legendary widows and orphans.

America is unique in this legal tax racketeering. Most industrialized nations have reduced dividend double taxation or eliminated it altogether.

Whatever happens, if Congress wants Americans to believe that taxes are fair (which they shouldn't because they're not), the government better do something to stop this legal extortion—fast.

Did you really say there's a 66 percent tax on dividends?

8

EARNED INCOME TAX CREDIT

Should We All Move to Boise?

Washington has had the middle class in its fiscal gun-sights for the longest time. Let's see how much we can take out of their pockets, say Washington tax experts, and give it away to everybody else.

To whom? It makes no difference as long as we hit the cash cow, the working families who make from $30,000 to $90,000 a year and pay most of the individual income taxes.

The latest wrinkle in this nefarious plan is the Earned Income Tax Credit, a gimmick that Washington propagandists have labeled a *boon* to taxpayers.

Let's say you live in Little Rock, Arkansas, and earn only $24,000 a year. Chances are you're not so bad off.

After all, even the full-time lieutenant governor of the state makes only $29,000.

You've got a $75,000 three-bedroom house and your property tax is only $950, a real laugher. (It's closer to $500 in the rest of the state.) You've got enough money for a decent life, even for a good $6 dinner.

Still, Uncle Sam feels sorry for you. In fact, you're eligible for a reverse tax—a burgeoning welfare program called Earned Income Tax Credit, which grants tax credits, *even delivers checks from the IRS*. This is not peanuts. The EITC bonanza will soon run as high as $3,370 per family and cost us $28 billion a year annually!

Is this government tax scheme, which was enormously expanded by President Clinton in 1994, just for the poorest of the poor?

Hardly. In fact, the Little Rock homeowner, who needs no federal handout, is included in the EITC dole. By 1996, it will go to families of four making as much as $27,000.

Is EITC just for a handful of Americans? Hardly. In 1995, credits and checks will go out to some 17 million American families—or some 55 million people. And beginning this year, families *without children and even single folks will be eligible*—the opposite of the family program's intent.

So what, you say? Isn't it a good idea that keeps the working poor off welfare?

That was the concept. It's OK at first glance, but the closer you get, the more it looks like a tax scandal that takes money from the already-drained middle class and moves it, wholesale, from one part of the country to the other, and from high-cost suburbs to cheaper rural areas, and even from one neighbor in a town to the other.

It's the biggest geographic transfer swindle in the history of the nation, and one of the many hidden taxes invented by Washington.

The truth is that the EITC money for the Arkansas family (and people in other low-cost, low-tax states) comes from the taxes and out of the pocket of the very same type of family, living in the same kind of house, but in a more expensive part of the country.

The new tax sucker may have a larger income on paper, but because of his higher cost of living, including higher local and state taxes, he's actually much poorer than many people getting EITC tax relief. He has a miserable fiscal existence, and he's the one paying for the EITC!

Let's look at the Smith family on Long Island, New York. They're making $33,000 a year, the average national household income, but they're not eligible for EITC. They live in the same size house as the family in Arkansas, but instead of costing $75,000, the house set them back $200,000. And instead of under $1,000 property taxes as in Little Rock, they're paying, so help me God, *six times as much*. They're also saddled with higher state income taxes.

Yet that New York suburbanite, who can't make ends meet, is dispatching some of his sweat money all around America, courtesy of the U.S. Congress, the president of the United States, and their faithful tool, the IRS, and its crazy tax code.

Go figure.

Who's going to pay for it all? Guess? The middle class, the true targets of the green eyeshade guys in the basement of the Treasury building.

In effect, Washington is ripping off Mr. and Mrs. Taxpayer in New York, Michigan, California, Massachusetts, New Jersey, Connecticut, et al., and sending it, in the greatest money transfer in American history, to families in the poorer states who may be living much better on much less. EITC is just the latest assault on the great, disappearing, abused American middle class.

The EITC program began quite modestly, as do most of Washington's nonsensical ideas. It started out reasonably in 1975 to help poor families pay their regressive Social Security taxes. The credit maximum was $400, welcome help for working people.

But now? Washington went into its usual overdrive, and EITC is the fastest growing of all federal programs. In 1982, it cost less than $2 billion. By 1988, it took $5.6 billion out of the treasury. In 1993, the tab was $15 billion—which is just the beginning. By 1996, it will cost $28 billion and still be growing!

Congress has continuously raised the eligibility income limits. In 1987, it was $15,432 for a family of four, then rose to $20,264 in 1990 and is now a ridiculous $27,000. This despite the fact that the typical American paycheck is only $25,000 a year.

With the continuous lifting of the income ceiling, millions flocked into EITC. From less than 2 million, it expanded to 15 million families by 1993, and will take in 21 million by 1996.

If we don't stop it, and its drain on the middle class,

*we can easily project that 35 million families, or some
100 million Americans, will be on this IRS dole by the
year 2000—taking tax money from the people just barely
above them in earnings, and often below them in pur-
chasing power.*

And the size of the EITC checks and credits are
growing apace. Just as recently as 1990, the EITC maximum given by the IRS was $953. In 1996, it will be
$3,370 a year per family and rising.

What if the EITC beneficiary wants to get his hand
on some of your tax money before the end of the year?
Easy. The new Clinton plan allows him to claim 60 percent of the credit, or cash, and have it added to his paycheck by the IRS.

Poverty has been defined by the Census Bureau as
$14,700 for a family of four. But when it comes to the
EITC, the limits are almost double that. Even the $14,700
poverty level is meaningless geographically. In rural Mississippi, you can eat fine on that. In a New York or Chicago suburb, you'd better get on a fast-moving soup
kitchen line.

And do people try to cheat on the EITC? You bet
they do, shamelessly.

The government rejects some 30 percent of claims
because they're not eligible. On top of that, EITC is the
largest center of fraud in the tax system. In 1995, the IRS
held up millions of tax refund checks while they took a
closer look for EITC connivers who purposely understate
their income.

Surprisingly, you don't even have to apply for EITC.
The IRS, which can hound middle-class taxpayers into a

nervous breakdown for $20, will graciously go over the tax return and send the filer a credit, or a check, without his ever asking for it!

How can we bring some reason to this asinine runaway program?

Easy as pie. We can be both compassionate and reasonable, and still make the ridiculous tax code saner.

1. Limit EITC tax welfare to *truly* poor families. Use the government's own poverty level of $15,000 as an upper limit. Let's not take tax money from people making $33,000 in high-income areas and give it to richer people making $27,000 in poorer areas.

2. Figure the poverty level state by state, as we do with some welfare programs. $20,000 might be the poverty level in the New York metropolitan area, and $10,000 in rural Arkansas, with $15,000 as an average. That will stop bleeding the budget and be fairer as well.

3. Generous (with your money) President Clinton has extended EITC to couples *without children*. That violates the spirit of the plan and should be discontinued immediately.

4. Cut out all EITC credits and payments to *single* people, a program now clicking in which will take more tax billions from middle-class families.

5. Eureka! We now learn that Washington has been sending EITC tax credits and cash to *illegal immigrants* all these years. Frightened by Proposition 187 in California, embarrassed former Treasury secretary Lloyd Bentsen stated that the IRS will try to eliminate the program for non-Americans. They should be cut off forthwith.

6. Here's a total solution to the whole EITC tax fiasco—one that will solve the tax problem of hard-pressed families with children, poor or middle class.

Immediately eliminate the EITC. Instead give every man, woman, and child an additional $2,500 personal deduction regardless of income, the system under Harry Truman. Forget the class-conscious means test and remember that we're all Americans.

That deduction will not only help poor families (a $10,000 deduction for four) more than the EITC, but it will stop the unfair transfer of money from the middle class, who can't take it anymore. And the way the EITC tax dole is growing, my plan will end up being cheaper.

Scream at your member of Congress. Tell him you want tax relief for everyone and not crazy tax transfers that always hit middle-class families the hardest.

What, you say, he doesn't listen? Just remind him of the 1994 election and that there's another one just like it coming up.

Do you have a personal alternative?

Yes, you can pack up, leave the high-cost, high-tax areas and move to Little Rock. Or better still, go to clean, low-cost Boise, Idaho, or even rural Montana, where life will be cheaper and better, if a little chillier in winter.

And until the president and the Congress regain their sanity, you might be able to get on the EITC tax dole yourself.

9

ENVIRONMENTAL TAXES

Recycle and Pay

As part of the world's second-oldest profession, tax collectors will always find a new excuse to pick the pockets of working people.

Today, it's the environment.

You mean you're not in favor of a cleaner planet?

Of course I am, but like many others, I am only willing to pay taxes for programs that are well-constructed. Otherwise, the burden on the people is going to exceed the gain. That's exactly what's beginning to happen with parts of the environmental plan.

There's little quarreling with requiring industry to clean up their act. They pay the tariff, as they should.

But government programs—whether directed by

Washington or Town Hall—are something else. With our taxes and fees we pay for schemes that are often misguided and mismanaged. The Superfund, for example, has cost us over $15 billion and has done little cleanup. Washington has also passed environmental bills that we've all applauded: the Clean Air Act and the Safe Drinking Water Act.

Who doesn't want clean air and water?

The problem is that although Washington has mandated these programs, it pays almost none of the bill. States and cities are forced to raise taxes to fulfill Washington's will, which is often stronger than it is bright.

Take Anchorage, Alaska. They've been working overtime to fulfill federal environmental mandates. But it's cost them $25 million a year, forcing cuts in other services. The city fathers estimate the cost in this decade to be $428 million, or $4,649 per household!

The environmental cost in Columbus, Ohio, borders on the catastrophic. They're up to $82 million a year for *only* federal projects. They figure the decade's cost at $1.6 billion. By the year 2000, just environmental costs will take 23 percent of the city's budget!

Localities are also piling up environmental tax bills by themselves.

One popular program is "curbside" pickup of recycled trash, which now involves one in three American households. That well-intentioned idea requires the hands-on separation of garbage into plastics, glass, tins, and newspapers, all laid out neatly for the garbageman.

Good idea, no?

No. It's not only costing taxpayers hundreds of millions a year, but it is virtually useless environmentally.

What?

How can you say that when our schoolchildren are being brought up on recycling? Talk of it brings enthusiastic huzzahs in social studies classes. But there's a problem. The whole idea is expensive and of little or no value environmentally.

San Jose, California, spends $5 million a year on curbside rituals. New York City faces a $100 million cost mandated by the court that it fulfill its own goal of recycling 25 percent of its garbage. Private-home collection fees have risen as towns require private garbagemen to handle home-sorted garbage.

Waste Age magazine reports that states now tax and spend $250 million a year just to subsidize recycling.

But why is it a bad idea, even if it costs a few hundred million?

Because the real recycling goes on in industry, where entrepreneurs (like the old junkmen) gather up waste and sell it to manufacturers. That costs the taxpayers nothing, makes industry more efficient, and takes up the lion's share of recycling.

But how about all the garbage coming out of the average home? Actually, it's only a drop in the dump.

Industrial nonhazardous waste involves 7 *billion* tons a year, and hazardous waste—a real problem—some 750 million tons. Consumer trash accounts for a measly 116 million tons, or less than 8 percent of all garbage. Household recycling is only 1 or 2 percent of the total, at the most.

Nor is there any economic gain in home recycling, despite the advertising. The price of old paper and plastics has rebounded some, but it still costs more to collect old Pepsi bottles and copies of the *Weekly Whatever* than it brings in. Towns are losing money and passing the cost on to homeowners in higher taxes and garbage fees.

(Collection drives and drop-in Dumpsters are more economical.)

One recycling consultant says that city councilmen are shocked to find out that home recycling programs cost, not make, money. "It's like moving from once-a-week garbage collection to twice a week," she has pointed out.

In Los Angeles, it's estimated that they would need only half their eight hundred garbage trucks if they stopped curbside pickup of recyclables.

So what if there's no money to be made in recycling? What if it even costs us money? At least we'll help to solve the garbage crisis.

What garbage crisis? The reality is that we have a landfill *surplus*, not a shortage. We can handle all the garbage that Americans can dispose of—at lower cost than we're now paying in environmental taxes.

The sight of the New York garbage barge circling the globe looking for a place to land accelerated the myth that there was no place to dump garbage. (The boat was really turned away because of unproven rumors that the garbage contained hazardous waste.)

The so-called landfill crisis never existed. Today's sanitary landfills, lined with clay or plastic, with a liquid runoff and control of methane gas, plus fresh layers of dirt to keep away scavengers, have a virtually unlimited capacity. They can be 20, 40, 100, or even 200 or 300 feet high and accomplish the same job more economically, and just as safely environmentally.

The U.S. Conference of Mayors says that the average city has 16.5 years of capacity remaining in garbage landfills. The major waste companies have 12.5 years left on their sites, with new capacity coming on-line all the time. Mid-American Waste Systems in Ohio boosted its dump to a 200-million-ton capacity from 20 million tons in only six years.

But some cities and towns insist on home recycling. To encourage the practice, several are even charging very high garbage collection fees. Known as "Pay as You Throw," cities like Seattle, Washington, and Lansing, Michigan, are charging homeowners for their garbage by the bag—$1.50 per in Lansing. Seattle boasts that as a result of the new tax, solid waste garbage has decreased almost 20 percent in a decade.

(Why not? If they charge $5 a bag, the homeowners will start to raise pigs.)

It's a strange tax, especially since curbside recycling is too small to make any environmental difference, and it's costing us an arm and a plastic jug.

BUT, schoolteachers remind us, what about the kids? Home recycling makes them feel so good.

I understand and sympathize. But perhaps they should spend less time on that and more time on Tom Jefferson and Ben Franklin. In the long run, they'll be much smarter and end up with a much better, low-taxed country.

Then they'll really feel good.

10

FLAT TAX

Confession on a Postcard

During the 1992 presidential campaign, Democratic hopeful Jerry Brown, former governor of California, advanced the idea of a "flat tax"—a federal income levy with no deductions, and all confessed to Uncle Sam on a postcard.

Each of us would just fill out a simple form and pay 10 percent of our gross income to Washington.

The response? There was "Governor Moonbeam" at it again, critics said, shooting at the lunar landscape, if you know what I mean.

Well, there's nothing as powerful as an idea whose time has come. And what the press brushed aside from Jerry Brown is now coming into vogue in the most respectable of circles.

It's not yet a tax, but it would be, so we should look at it closely.

No one less than Dick Armey, the Republican Majority Leader of the House, is pushing the flat tax idea. His starting rate is 20 percent, dropping to 17 percent in the third year of the new system, but he eliminates a lot of other taxes along the way.

Not to be outdone, House Minority Leader Democrat Dick Gephardt quickly joined the choir, announcing his own unflat version of the flat tax. He would start at 10 percent and go up progressively depending on income, which, of course, violates the whole idea of a flat tax. But that's politics in the good old U.S. of A.

What, really, is the appeal of the flat tax? As Dick Armey keeps pointing out, you can file on a postcard because there are no deductions. That sounds good, and brings up the pleasant spectre of getting H & R Block or the more expensive CPAs off your payroll. Life would be gentler and April 15 would lose its deadly psychological pall—maybe.

Dick Armey, a bright former professor of economics, tries to balance the lack of deductions with large personal exemptions that would take millions of lower-middle-class families off the tax roles. That includes $26,200 for a married couple filing jointly, plus $5,300 for each child, which gives a family of four a $36,800 exemption before they pay a penny to Uncle Sam.

Taxes will be evened out for everybody else, and almost the entire mess we call the Tax Code will be thrown out. Corporations will pay the same 17–20 percent as me and you (they now pay about 34 percent) and dividends will not be double taxed. Inheritance taxes will be eliminated, as will all loopholes. Business will surely increase, as will the Gross Domestic Product.

Sound like Nirvana? It is. But in some ways it isn't.

Why? Well, we'll still have an income tax and the IRS with its probing and harassment. And millions will still have to keep receipts and books to find out what to confess to on the postcard.

Besides simplicity, the advantage of the flat tax is the lower rate and the absence of deductions. The disadvantage, of course, is the absence of deductions.

Why? Simply because it badly penalizes millions of Americans in high-tax, high-cost areas. In fact, the flat tax has the same built-in geographic penalty as the Earned Income Tax Credit. And here we're talking really big bucks.

It's nice to think about America as one homogeneous country, but the reality is far from that.

For Instance I. A family in suburban New York or California has to pay high state income taxes, which are no longer deductible. So they would pay higher "flat" taxes than others.

For Instance II. A family in many suburban areas— from Minneapolis to Cleveland to Los Angeles and San Francisco—where homes cost $250,000 or more, would tend to have larger mortgages. Since they could no longer deduct the mortgage interest, they'd have larger "flat" taxes than people in low-cost areas with lower home prices and smaller mortgages.

(Another danger. The loss of mortgage interest deductions would lower the value of homes. BEWARE. We don't want to hurt home equity, which represents almost the entire net worth of most families.)

For Instance III. People who live in high–property tax areas—anywhere between $5,000 and $20,000 a year—would no longer be able to deduct that abusive local tax on their postcard, so they too would pay larger "flat" taxes come April 15.

For Instance IV. Better American school districts, which often pay astronomical teaching salaries (Irvington, New York, a suburb of the Big Apple, has a median teacher compensation of $67,500!) have astronomical school taxes to match. Those lofty school taxes would no longer be deductible on the 1040, forcing them to pay higher "flat" taxes, which would be unfair.

In simple summary, the flat tax will favor people in low-tax, low-cost states and communities with low-price homes. The tax may be flat, but it won't be even, sort of like an old, warped table.

What can we do to fix the flat tax and still keep its elimination of the mad Internal Revenue Tax Code?

I hereby formally propose the answer to Congress. It's a simple one which I'll modestly label "The Armey-Gross Almost-Flat Tax." It will carry all his provisions, except for three:

1. We should retain the home mortgage interest deduction.

2. We should retain the state and local tax deduction.

3. We will keep the corporate income tax as is, using the money for the above deductions.

Armey's personal allowances are pretty attractive, but they too have a problem—a deep geographic bias. Under his plan a family of four has an automatic deduction of $36,800. The majority of people in low-cost, low-income areas and states will pay no income taxes at all.

Sounds good, but without the deductions I've suggested, the IRS burden will be shifted to the citizens of high-tax, high-cost-of-living, high-income states such as New York, Connecticut, Ohio, Michigan, New Jersey, California, et al. Molto pericoloso, *as Italians are prone to say when danger is almost upon them.*

There's one other idiosyncrasy of the Armey plan. So that people will feel the acute pain of paying taxes, Armey wants to cut out pay-as-you-go payroll withholding and have taxpayers send in a monthly check to Uncle Sam.

Lots of luck. All we'll get is millions more delinquent taxpayers, with penalties and interest up to you know where.

But the Armey plan does have many merits, and it's gaining support among noteworthy tax organizations.

If Mr. Armey will yield to joint authorship (without credit to me, if he likes) of a plan that adds those vital deductions and changes I've just suggested, I believe we will have begun the *first* step toward eliminating the curse of the Sixteenth Amendment.

I await Mr. Armey's phone call and a fruitful collaboration for America, one to which I have always responded.

(Don't worry, Dick. It'll just take a slightly larger postcard.)

The second step, of course, is the one in which the flag will wave even higher—that's the closing of the IRS, the day America will become truly free.

Still, a federal income tax return on a postcard doesn't sound half bad, does it?

11

GAMBLING TAX

Curiouser and Curiouser

If you're a professional gambler working in a state where it's legal, life with the IRS is easy. You pay them $50 a year registration fee, plus one-quarter of one percent of all your transactions.

For example, if a gambler in Las Vegas handles $10 million in sports bets a year, he pays Uncle Sam $25,000, which won't break his bank. (Those who don't register we call "bookies," from the book they keep to write down wagers.)

But the story gets more complicated when you're just an ordinary player at a casino. Then it takes on an Alice in Wonderland quality so typical of the IRS.

A high roller walks into a Las Vegas casino and

plunks down $15,000 for chips. Following IRS regulations, the casino fills out a Cash-In slip that says the player started with $15,000. When the amount is over $10,000, a CTR, or Cash Transaction Report, goes to the IRS. The player then moves to the baccarat table (shades of James Bond) and plays for seven hours.

The result? He wins $100,000 and leaves with a smile on his face.

What about his federal income tax, which the government requires all Americans to pay on gambling profits? Does the government collect?

There's the rub.

"The casino fills in a Cash-In CTR—which is one way of slowing down money laundering—and that goes to us," says an IRS gaming expert. "But by Nevada state law, the casino's not required to fill out a Cash-Out CTR slip. They're exempt. So although we know what he started with from the Cash-In CTR, we have no way of knowing how much the gambler's won. He's obligated by law to report the winnings on his own income tax return, but we're completely in the dark about what really happened at the gaming tables."

I was surprised. "What was the philosophy behind that?" I asked.

"It's simple. We're not really after the players," the IRS expert responded. "We assume that his winnings are a flash in the pan. Win tonight, lose tomorrow. Since the casinos in Las Vegas make enough money to build their giant establishments, the odds are obviously very heavy in their favor. So we assume that the gambler who walks out with $100,000 one night will give it all back some other night. We figure he really hasn't won anything overall."

Strange logic, but there it is.

Or is it?

Actually, the government can be quite strict about other types of gambling winnings and makes sure you pay your taxes on them.

"The rule is that if the odds are 300 to 1 or more— like some slot-machine payoffs, lotteries, football pools, pari-mutuel bets—then the winner is given a W2-G [for gambling] form," the IRS man explained. "In the case of slots, he's given a W2-G if the take is $1,200 or more."

The cut-off point—where the IRS requires a report and deducts 28 percent withholding—varies with the game. In bingo, a $1,200 win also requires immediate IRS reporting, while it's $1,500 in keno, and $10,000 in poker pools.

Does the IRS ever watch the gaming tables to spot a big winner at dice, for instance?

"No, contrary to rumor, we never watch the players. We sometimes put undercover people in the cage to check for skimming and look out for money laundering. But we don't watch players. We really don't care about them."

But what about that $100,000 baccarat (or dice) winner who hasn't reported his winnings to the IRS? Is he less important than the silver-haired matron from Kansas City who's broken the bank by winning $1,200 in bingo?

Apparently yes, even if the logic of it escapes us.

Is this somewhat nonchalant attitude of the IRS toward Las Vegas the rule throughout the United States?

Not exactly. Surprisingly, in other casinos, the big winners are reported to the IRS on the spot.

"Nevada's state law doesn't require a Cash-Out slip, so we go along with them," he explains. "But in the case of Atlantic City, Indian casinos, riverboats in Illinois, Missouri, Indiana, Mississippi, Louisiana, and the new land-based casinos going up in New Orleans and probably Bridgeport, Connecticut, the casino will fill out a CTR for both Cash-In over $10,000 and a Cash-Out. There we'll know exactly what high-rollers won that night."

Curiouser and curiouser.

What happens to the CTR for big winners?

"The Cash Transaction Reports are turned over to us and put into a central computer file," the IRS man explained. "If one of those big winners is audited, we'll check the CTR file and his return to see if he's reported the gains."

And if not?

Well, the IRS said, the winner could explain that he lost an equal amount or more over time, and therefore was not required to pay a tax.

How does he do that, I asked, now more perplexed than ever.

"He can try to prove the loss by keeping a diary as he goes along, or by getting a letter from the casino manager that he's a regular customer and usually loses," our IRS expert explained. "But if he can't prove the loss and we have a CTR on his gains, say from Atlantic City, then he'll have to pay income tax on the winnings."

So? Does that mean that Las Vegas winnings are less

of a concern for the IRS than money won elsewhere? Or of less interest than the keno winnings of a matron from Dubuque?

Apparently, yes. Which only proves that when it comes to taxes and the IRS, anything can happen, and generally does.

What is my advice?

(1) Don't gamble; (2) if you do, keep it small; (3) try not to get lucky enough to earn a CTR; and (4) if you must win, do it in Las Vegas.

Still, you're better off if you stick to bingo. At least if you win, you know you've paid your taxes.

Only in America.

12

GASOLINE TAX

How Uncle Sam Steals Our Pump Money

The next time you pump your self-service gas, take a look at the price.

Remember that 18.4 cents on a gallon goes to Uncle Sam, and another 19 cents, on average, to your state.

What's it for?

My God, we've been told that over and over again. *All* that federal tax money goes to build America's excellent interstate highways and keep them in good repair.

Noble motive. And it's true, isn't it?

Not really. In reality, the gas tax is one of Washington's most ingenious swindles. Supposedly, it's all for roads, but in fact, a multibillion-dollar piece—what gamblers call "vigorish"—is taken out by Uncle Sam every day to feed the monster called Washington.

Some of your gas tax money goes to highways and roads, but much less of it than you think.

We're talking big bucks. According to the Tax Foundation, the federal tax from gasoline (and gasohol) brought in $22 billion in 1994, not counting almost $5 billion more from diesel fuel. Uncle Sam knows gas is as essential to Americans as McDonald's, and uses that fact to tap the pipeline from your pocket to the Treasury Building on 14th and Pennsylvania.

Lately, he's been tapping it on a regular basis. In recent years, Washington has raised the gas tax three times, from a measly 4 cents a gallon in 1982 to 9 cents in 1983 to 14 cents in 1984 to 18.4 cents in 1994 (a 425 percent hike). The last gas tax rise was part of Bill Clinton's supposed balancing of the budget in the never-never future.

Once an incidental amount, gas taxes, both federal and state, will reach $50 billion in 1995, or some $500 per household. To the couple making $100,000 it's not crippling, but this most regressive of all taxes hits the working man where it hurts. And it annoys the hell out of the pressured middle class.

Typically, as soon as the federal government increases taxes, the states jump to follow suit. After the last federal rise, thirteen states did the same. Most states have high gas taxes, with Connecticut the champion with a 31-cent-a-gallon levy. The lowest is Georgia with only 7.5 cents, followed by Alaska, Wyoming, and New Jersey, where the tax is a relatively low 10.5 cents.

The trucking companies also contribute, if without

their permission. The tax on heavy tires over fifty pounds, plus trucks and trailer-use taxes, bring in $2.4 billion a year. (Trucking costs go up to boot.)

Where does all the gas money go?

As I've said, some of it goes to the roads, but billions more are taken from our gas taxes and used for everything from monthly checks to unwed mothers to twenty-nine limos for the White House to virtually free water for millionaire California farmers.

How does this tax racket, one of the biggest of all time, work?

Very simply.

The federal government will take a fortune this year from your 18.4 cents at the pump. From that, 11.5 cents will go into the Highway Trust Fund. What about the rest?

The law says it's for "deficit reduction," a funnymoney euphemism for wasteful spending. The reality is that of every dollar in gas taxes, 37 cents goes directly into the General Fund, where it is spent on everything except highways.

How much is diverted in that fashion? Some $7 billion in 1995. Since 1983, $40 billion has been taken from our gas taxes to pay the bills of the bloated Washington establishment.

That's only the beginning of the Beltway sleight of hand. The rest of the gas tax receipts are then put into the Highway Trust Fund (you should excuse the expression), where it's supposed to sit awaiting its use on the road.

But that envisions a trustworthy federal government. On December 31, 1994, there was $17.7 billion in the kitty, or there *appeared* to be. In reality, you could turn the "trust fund" over on its macadam and not a nickel would drop out.

The entire gas "trust fund" has been borrowed by Uncle Sam. What collateral has he given? The fund has been given pieces of paper—Special Certificates of Indebtedness—federal IOUs which have become part of the $4.9 trillion debt, which no one in *mens sana* believes will ever be paid back.

In addition to taking 37 cents on each dollar out of gas taxes for use elsewhere, the government treats the remaining money in the trust fund like a piggybank. It is guaranteed, say the politicians, by the "full faith and credit" of the U.S. government. That means they have the right to borrow still more money to pay back what they borrowed from the fund in the first place.

Or, they'll raise the gas taxes again, and again, something I can predict without any fear of contradiction.

What is there to do?

Simple.

1. Congress should pass legislation requiring that all gas taxes and other highway fees go *solely* into the highway and road system.

2. Build and repair still more roads or drastically lower the gas tax.

3. By law, prohibit the federal government from "borrowing" our gas taxes, which we eventually have to pay back to ourselves anyway.

So the next time you fill up, remember that almost half your taxes at the pump goes to everything in the world except your roads.

The EPA requires a notice at service stations that the gas fumes can be dangerous to your health. Maybe we should put another sticker right on the pump:

BEWARE. GAS TAXES CAN BE HARMFUL TO YOUR POCKETBOOK.

13

HOTEL AND TRAVEL TAXES

The Government Killjoy

Politicians may be sneaky, but they're not stupid.

They know that when you're on the move, either for business or on holiday, you're a little looser with your cash than usual. Taxi fares of $25 from the airport are more than you'd contemplate when you had your feet—and your mind—solidly on ground.

Knowing this, clever tax people have made travel very taxing, to say the least. They have a solid base to begin with. Americans make 1.1 billion trips a year, and the travel industry is the second-largest employer in America, and the third-largest retail business.

By tapping into this giant market, various governments—federal, state, and local—are able to collect

$52 billion in travel taxes, a disproportionate amount for any business and equal to 14 cents on each dollar spent for travel.

And they get away with it. Why? Because you're a captive and vulnerable audience when you travel. Who's going to go home just because of high taxes as you move across the country, or the world? And who are you going to complain to? It's probably not your home state or city.

Travel taxes are atrocious, even unconscionable. We've already seen the exorbitant tax on airline traffic, but that's outdone by lodging taxes. A recent study of hotel taxes in the Big Apple, for example, shows that for rooms of $100 or more a night, visitors had been paying an average $25 in taxes!

Not to be outdone, Washington, D.C.—where good rooms run some $200 a night—not only has a 13 percent hotel tax, but adds a surcharge of $1.50 "bed tax" on top of that. (If you sleep on the floor, do they take it off your bill?)

Virtually every major city in America has a double-digit hotel/lodging tax. It runs 15 percent and more in Columbus, Ohio; Houston; and Seattle. Chicago charges 14.86 percent; Cleveland 14.50; Memphis 13.25; San Antonio 13; St. Louis 13.85. New Orleans, which has an 11 percent lodging tax, makes up for it by adding a daily room surcharge.

A cornucopia of governments look to your perambulations to make a quick buck. In some cities, visitors pay five taxes on their rooms: state occupancy tax, city occupancy tax, state sales tax, city sales tax, and a "bed" surcharge. A check of the top fifty cities shows that only six have a single-digit tax rate, and most of those are at 9 percent.

When the total room tax reaches the dreaded "2" number, or 20 percent, it can also bring a groan not only from tourists but from the hotels, fearful of a lower-tax competition.

High-tax New York, which books the largest number of visitors, tries to cash in on out-of-towners by ripping them off, tax-wise. The tax on a $200 room had (1) a base state sales tax of 8.25 percent, (2) a special occupancy tax of 5 percent on rooms costing $100 or more, (3) a city hotel occupancy tax of 6 percent, and (4) a city room occupancy tax (bed tax) of $2 on rooms of $40 or more. Lower rates than that puts you on Skid Row.

The total tax on a $200-a-night room? $44.50! On an average $113 room, the tax was over $24. Believe it or not.

Out-of-towners believed it and quietly began to boycott the Big Apple as a tourist spot. After the last 5 percent tax was imposed in 1990, business started to level off, then drop. It's called economics.

The result? After that last raise, the New York tourist association found that two years later, they *lost* more than $94 million in hotel tax revenues. Another study showed that twenty prime hotels in New York were up for sale partly because travel taxes were cutting visitor trade. Sixty-four conventions turned down New York bids in retaliation for their fleecing of tourists.

The rule is inflexible: The larger the tax the smaller the business.

Did the money at least go to promote tourism as some communities claim?

Lots of luck. Of the exorbitant New York hotel tax, only 1 percent went for that good purpose. The rest went into the general fund to pay politicians' salaries, welfare, and you name it.

New York is finally waking up to their suicidal error. Mayor Rudy Giuliani recently removed the city occupancy tax of 6 percent on hotels, lowering the tariff to 13.25 percent plus the daily surcharge of $2. It's still too high, but he hopes it's not too late to turn things around.

Hotel taxes are also tacked on to get visitors to involuntarily support local booster causes. It's a sneaky kind of operation. The New Orleans hotel tax includes 4 percent for the Superdome, which Kansas City people couldn't care less about.

Chicago's hotel tax goes into its bloated general fund, but a 2.14 percent Illinois sports facility authority occupancy tax pays for the new Comiskey Park for the Chicago Cubs. Local hotel people complain that few out-of-towners go to the ballgame, so why should they shoulder the tax burden?

Cleveland has added a 1.5 percent hotel tax to pay for the construction of a Rock and Roll Hall of Fame, paid for by many aging fans of Frank Sinatra who couldn't care less.

The hotel hit is only part of the total travel burden. Gas taxes are high, as we've seen, as are airplane levies. Two other taxes that travelers complain about are restaurant meal taxes and high taxes on car rentals, another captive audience.

Meal taxes in the fifty major markets range from *no* tax at all in Portland, Oregon, to 10 percent in Minneapolis, with 7.5 percent being typical, and many higher than the local sales tax.

The loudest growls are reserved for car rental taxes and fees. First there is the combined local and state car rental taxes, which rival those of hotels.

In Minneapolis, it's 12.7 percent of your car rental bill, and a little higher in Chicago, plus a surcharge of $2.75 a day. As usual, New York is up there with the leaders, with an 8.25 percent sales tax rate, plus a 5 percent car rental surcharge, or 13.25 percent. Baltimore charges car rentees 11.5 percent, while Denver is 11, Reno 12.5, Houston 12, and Seattle 11.5.

In addition to the regular rental tax, every city in Ohio adds a $4-a-day surcharge. Pennsylvania adds $2 a day, and Florida, to top them, $2.05.

Because the car rentee is seen as a supreme sucker, there's one tax abuse that's more than annoying. That's the hit placed on customers who rent cars *off* airport grounds, and have to pay a fee to have a shuttle take them to and fro.

Sometimes, it's quite reasonable: $2.98 in Denver; $3.10 in Fort Lauderdale; $1.75 in Minneapolis.

BUT some towns play the highwayman with those unfortunates who rented a car at off-airport premises. Then the tax becomes virtual blackmail if you want to make your plane back home. *In Tampa, for example, they have to pay a penalty of 10 percent of the entire bill—$30 on a $300 bill—just to be shuttled to their plane.*

These atrocious "fees" are collected by the car rental

company, but they're not used to pay for the bus shuttle. They're actually a tax that goes to support the semi-governmental municipal airport.

The tax is generally an exorbitant 7 or 8 percent of the bill (West Palm Beach), and goes up to 10 percent not only in Tampa but in Sacramento, Knoxville, and Atlanta as well. In Las Vegas, the combined local tax plus the off-airport fee comes to 20.5 percent of the entire car rental bill!

"People yell about it," says a car rental agent in Tampa (16.5 percent tariff plus $2.05 a day), "but there's nothing they can do about it."

Should we stop traveling?

No one says you shouldn't travel. It's good for the soul if dangerous for the pocketbook.

But if you do, be aware that you're being ripped off, day in and day out.

The American tourist is the perfect class-A target of the tax writers who know a marvelous moving mark when they see one.

14

INCOME TAX, STATE AND CITY

Little Uncle Sams

If you're raging mad at Uncle Sam on April 15, please save a little bile for the Statehouse, and even for your hometowns.

Not long after 1913, when the Sixteenth Amendment made the rape of our paychecks constitutional, several states decided to cut themselves into the Income Tax Racket. It's the easiest way for politicians to separate citizens from their cash, and the most painful for tax-payers.

It's right off the top, like making a large bank loan payment for the rest of your life.

Today, of course, it's routine in forty-three states, Connecticut having joined the tide in 1991. There are still seven holdouts—Alaska, Florida, Nevada, South Dakota, Texas, Washington, and Wyoming.

Income-tax-less Florida and Texas prove that people vote with their feet. Both states are among the fastest growing in the nation, while high income tax areas like New York and Connecticut are losing population and jobs with Olympian speed.

State income tax rates range all over the lot, creating emotions from simple sighs to spitting anger.

The champions are California, where income tax rates rise to 11 percent; the District of Columbia, which reaches 9.5 percent; Hawaii with a top bracket of 10 percent; Iowa near 10 percent; Montana with 11 percent; New Mexico with 8.5 percent; Oregon with 9 percent.

(Some states like Connecticut—which charges 4.5 percent—seem to have a low rate, but they're just fooling the public. Connecticut doesn't allow taxpayers to use most federal deductions like mortgage interest, so their true rate is close to 7 percent.)

Many citizens have become savvy about spending and waste in Washington, but most don't know about state profligacy, another insidious public disease. Some costs have been forced on them by Washington, but many states have tried to ape Beltway largesse. If Uncle Sam is a drunken sailor, the fifty states are on a Lost Weekend.

All government spending rose an astronomical 480 percent from 1950 to 1990. But the Statehouses outdid them all—rising by 534 percent! The last decade was among the worst. From 1980 to 1990, *state spending grew four times as fast as population growth, and 60 percent more than inflation*. Today, the total state tax bill—

not counting local taxes—is reaching toward $700 billion
a year.

The state tax burden now averages $4,000 per
household, including small single-person households,
with some states like New York ($5,000), Connecticut
($5,500), Hawaii ($7,700), Alaska ($11,500), and
statelike District of Columbia ($11,000) leading the pack.
For a family of four the burden is at least 50 percent
higher.

State taxes are among the fastest-growing hits on our
pocketbook. In 1984, they rose a crushing 14.8 percent,
with an average increase of 7.6 percent from 1983 to
1993. Anyone who studied compound interest in the
ninth grade knows how those numbers can explode the
family budget.

Why so much state taxation?

There are many reasons, but the major ones are:

1. The constantly rising cost of welfare, pushed by
federal programs. In 1995, states will pay $110 billion for
their share of welfare. Just Medicaid, medical care for the
poor, now costs over $150 billion a year, some $70 billion of which is picked up by the states. Little wonder we
face higher state taxes.

2. States put up matching funds for 606 different
federal grants, for everything from job training programs
to dance.

3. States pay to carry out 175 different federal unfunded mandates, including prisons, Motor Voter, Americans with Disabilities, Clean Air and Safe Drinking
Water. (The new unfunded mandate law is far from pro-
hibitive, and it's not retroactive anyway.)

Uncle Sam's contribution? Nothing. Nada. Rien.

4. The rising cost of education (see "School Taxes") and crime control.

5. An orgy of state government growth in the 1980s when it looked like there was no tomorrow. Then tomorrow came.

6. The excess number of state civilian employees. Their ranks have gone up twice as fast as the population and now number over 2.7 million—in addition to the 2.2 million working for counties, and millions more for cities and towns.

The state's portion of the federal welfare package is crippling. In Connecticut, welfare costs are now $2.5 billion, more than a fourth of the entire budget. Though the state is bleeding jobs, they continue to lead the nation in shoveling money to unwed mothers. The average AFDC cash stipend is almost $600 a month, rising to some $1,000 in some wealthier areas of Fairfield County. (There Washington subsidizes rent for welfare families up to $1,710 a month!)

What's the hope for the fifty states?

First, Washington has to get off their backs. Block grants are a good idea because states can cut back their matching funds and put sensible schemes into place.

Some, like Wisconsin and Massachusetts, are already taking able-bodied men off the welfare rolls. Three states, starting with New Jersey, no longer give unwed mothers extra money for extra children. New Jersey is already witnessing a sizeable drop in out-of-wedlock births.

Some states are in open revolt against Washington. Three governors have refused to pay for Washington's pet project, the Motor Voter law. With unprecedented and arrogant action, Attorney General Janet Reno is suing them!

(This could prove a constitutional crisis. If a governor refuses to follow Washington's edict, can they arrest the head of a sovereign state? Stay tuned.)

Another revolt is brewing, this time in Texas. That state is refusing to enforce Washington's Clean Air Act when it comes to car pollution tests, which have to be paid for locally. A half dozen other states are also up in arms. Send a check or shut up, they're warning Uncle Sam. Of this, real (peaceful) revolutions are made.

The states are cutting back on aid to school districts, which only puts more burden on localities. The answer? Cut school budgets dramatically (see "School Taxes").

States are trying to slow down the growth in government, but that's far from sufficient. ZERO GROWTH IS THE ONLY ANSWER TO STATE BUDGET AND INCOME TAX PROBLEMS.

Governor Whitman of New Jersey has cut the state income tax by 30 percent, but the state's 1995–96 budget will still rise 3.5 percent. It's better than President Clinton's 1996 budget, which rises 4.5 percent, some 50 percent above inflation—if all goes his way, which is doubtful.

Mayor Giuliani of New York is trying to bring in a zero growth budget, the first since the Depression. Governor John Rowland of Connecticut is making a good effort, which may or may not work, as is Governor George Pataki of New York. Both states are in such perpetual financial crises that it will take even deeper cuts *every year for a decade* to get them out of the strangling tax morass.

Real slimming down of the number of employees in all states can be done by attrition—without layoffs—over a period of five years. And I promise that you won't notice that they're gone.

Voters in many states are pressing for laws, not promises, to curtail spending. They're called TELs, an acronym for Tax and Expenditure Limitations. It started in the late 1970s following the Howard Jarvis tax revolt in California, then slowed down. Recently, they've picked up as citizen activism in the Second American Revolution has soared.

As of today, twenty-four states have TELs. They work differently in each state, and some caps on taxes and spending are more effective than others. But overall, the results are reasonable and getting better.

In TEL states, from Delaware to Hawaii, spending per capita was above the national average before the law was enacted. But in the five years since TEL became law, spending dropped to 3 percentage points *below* the national average.

Several states are joining the TEL crusade. In March 1992, Oklahoma passed a constitutional amendment requiring that all tax increases either get voter approval or the agreement of three-fourths of the legislators. In November 1992, Colorado passed its Taxpayer Bill of Rights requiring voter approval for any tax increase. (It also limits spending growth to the rate of inflation.)

In Arizona, 72 percent of the voters approved a state constitutional amendment requiring a two-thirds vote in the legislature for any increase in taxes or fees. Washington State has also set a limit on spending.

You get the idea:

1. The first goal is to convince your state legislators and governor to put in an enforceable state spending cap.

2. The second goal is to convince your legislators and governor to reduce, then totally eliminate, the state income tax.

3. The third goal is to make it difficult (super-majority in legislature or voter approval) to raise taxes or fees.

4. If you don't have the Initiative in your state, go fight the legislature and the governor until you get it. (I'm helping to do that in my state.)

5. If you live in one of the twenty-four states that already has the Initiative, for God's sake, use it! Put an anti–income tax proposition on your ballot, and join the seven income tax–free states.

(Remember, we also need a constitutional amendment to level the playing field by granting the initiative to voters in all fifty states.)

And while our attention has been focused on the states, our cities and towns have been getting into the income tax racket as well.

Everyone knows about the over 4 percent income tax hit in the Big Apple, but what most don't know is that forty large cities in America and 3,500 local governments of all descriptions now have an income tax as well.

It's authorized for local governments in fourteen states—Alabama, California, Delaware, Indiana, Iowa, Kentucky, Maryland, Michigan, Missouri, New Jersey,

New York (where Yonkers joins New York City in the racket), Ohio, Oregon, and Pennsylvania—plus the District of Columbia.

Sadly, it all began in Philadelphia in 1938, where the income tax is now a punishing 5 percent. Then it spread throughout the nation, rising to 11 percent in the bankrupt District of Columbia. San Francisco and Los Angeles have it as well, but there it's called a "payroll tax" to soften the blow.

All these cities—like the income tax states—operate on the false theory that the more revenue the better the services, and therefore they'll attract people and jobs.

This is the great fallacy of the tax racket. Stephen Moore and Dean Stansel of the Cato Institute found that it really works backwards. From 1965 to 1990, the cities that took in the highest revenue per capita lost 10 percent of their jobs. Meanwhile, the leanest tax cities had over a 200 percent job growth. The same was true of population—people fled the high-tax cities in droves.

The fight against the tax racket continues daily, but if you're impatient until victory comes, you might want to take immediate personal action.

You can rent a moving van—as millions are already doing—and make the trek from California to New Hampshire (lowest tax burden) and from everywhere else to Texas (forty-ninth) or Florida (forty-sixth).

The option is yours.

Stay and fight or cut and run. Either way, you'd better do something before the state and local tax bill, now a trillion dollars, reaches the federal mark and we're all fiscally blown away.

15

INHERITANCE TAXES

Your Friendly Federal Undertaker

You work all your life to make a bundle to pass on to your children.

And what happens?

You meet this guy along the way—his name is IRS—and you get mugged on the day you die, fiscally speaking that is.

Americans have accepted as normal the idea that if you're successful and accumulate a million, or even less, that the federal government and your state are entitled to become partners of your heirs when you die.

Why?

Nobody knows. Some say it was to break up the accumulation of great wealth, dynasties that could destroy the democratic instinct of the nation—like the Rockefellers or the Morgans or the Carnegies. Sounds good, but there are so few of these plutocrats today that the idea is ludicrous. Only 245 estates of $20 million and over were handled by the IRS in a recent year.

The whole idea of an inheritance tax had always been considered un-American, and we never really had one until 1916.

We started the inheritance tax to help build the navy in 1797, then decided against it and repealed it in 1802. It was put in briefly for two emergencies, the Civil War and the Spanish-American War, but thrown out each time soon after.

Now our congressmen have forgotten America's natural inclination against robbing the dead. Despite the absence of any national emergency, they've instituted a tax that makes no economic sense.

Called a "transfer tax," the IRS euphemism for fiscal undertaking, it hits heavily those involved. In fact, it's the nation's steepest tax. After a $600,000 exemption, which hasn't been changed since 1987, the present tax starts at 37 percent and rises to 55 percent at $3 million. At $10 million, you lose the $600,000 exemption. They also add a 5 percent penalty for making so much money while you were alive! (Watch out, John Grisham.)

It was scheduled to go down to 50 percent in 1993, but President Clinton supported Congress in retaining the present exorbitant rate.

But strangely, if you're in the dynasty range—that's an estate of over $21 million—the penalty is dropped. Is there a begrudging respect for the *real, real rich* in Congress?

In addition, there's a state inheritance tax in twenty-six states, which can run as high as 20 percent, putting most of your estate in some government's bank account.

But the hard-working guy who leaves his children a house worth a half million dollars plus another half million in his pension plan is no Rockefeller and in no danger of starting a dynasty of plutocrats.

Avaricious Uncle Sam just wants his money. The *only* reason the IRS is there to take your family's wealth is because Congress believes they can get away with it. Naturally they want any nickel they can lay their hands on to feed the Washington monster. But in the case of a junior millionaire, or someone with less than that, inheritance taxes make no sense sociologically.

It is not a real redistribution of wealth, because we're dealing in small amounts. Neither does the federal government exemption of $600,000 mean that it's necessarily in liquid assets. That could just be the appraiser's evaluation of your estate, including your home, your antique jewelry, your furnishings, even your copper pots and pans from France. (We're talking real grave robbing.)

Nor is the inheritance tax based on any great theory—free market, socialist, or otherwise.

It's just a ghoulish practice by Uncle Sam that drives families mad; sets up internecine arguments between brothers, sisters, and cousins; destroys family businesses that have to be sold while they're thriving; and makes all the survivors nervous and despondent—even more so after the death of a loved one.

If, for example, most of an estate of a million dollars is in the value of a house, the heirs will probably have to sell it to satisfy the IRS bill.

What if real estate is soft? Or what if the stock market is way down and you'll have to take a bath? Will the IRS accept the tax in "kind"?

No way. It's strictly a cash business. They'll give you nine months to sell the assets, and you'll probably have to dump some, which is of little concern to the government. If a closely held business is part of the estate, they might give you an extension—while you pay the IRS interest. But they won't accept a deed to a house, or jewelry, or paintings—even though they'll tax them at full value.

This greedy nine-month rule came back to haunt one of its writers, Senator Robert Kerr of Oklahoma, a long-time member of the Senate Finance Committee. He died leaving an estate of $20 million. Upon his death the IRS asked his heirs for $9 million. They didn't have it, and liquidating his assets would mean a substantial loss. They raised $3 million, then borrowed $6 million, on which they had to pay interest with after-tax money. When it was all over, much of the estate was gone—to the bankers and the IRS.

(Sweet retribution!)

I asked a staffer at the House Ways and Means Committee, which also writes the tax laws, why we have an inheritance tax.

He was stymied for a minute. "Our present chairman doesn't believe in it, but I suppose the people who wrote the legislation wanted to redistribute the wealth through the tax laws. I personally don't think it makes any sense."

Does the government desperately need that deathbed money?

Hardly. Even with the handful of super-millionaires who die off (despite their best investment advice), the whole operation brings in *only three-quarters of 1 percent of the federal budget, less than we spend on farm subsidies.*

Several economists have concluded that the inheritance tax loses more money than it takes in. Like the income levy, say economists Patrick Fleenor and J. D. Foster of the Tax Foundation, "the estate tax discourages productive effort and saving," and is a disincentive to entrepreneurship.

Dr. Richard E. Wagner, an economist at George Mason University, believes the tax is taken from us at great social cost. According to him, "eliminating federal transfer taxes would improve the performance of the United States economy, strengthen family-owned businesses, and increase government revenues." What they raise, he says, is far exceeded by the lost Gross Domestic Product, jobs, and wages.

But what a federal fuss is made over it. An entire industry of estate planners, lawyers, accountants, insurance men have sprung up with gimmicks and trusts to try to beat Washington before it beats you all the way to the grave.

Of course, you can avoid the IRS *temporarily*. There is no "transfer tax" if you leave all your money to a spouse. They are exempt from both the gift and inheritance taxes, and assets can be transferred back and forth freely between spouses while they are alive—if they're U.S. citizens.

Why is Uncle Sam so lenient? It's simple arithmetic. The typical spouse is less than three years different in age to the other. Washington (and the states) can wait a while until the second one dies. Who knows? The estate might even be larger when Der Tag comes. Of course, they're a little concerned if a widower marries a spring chicken, who has fifty good tax-free years left in her bones.

But what if you want to generation-skip—leave your assets to your grandchildren? Perhaps you have no spouse, and your children are well fixed or maybe you never liked them to begin with. (Remember "How sharper than a serpent's tooth?")

Since the IRS is going to have to wait another generation until they rob the younger people's graves, Uncle Sam has figured out a retribution.

You can leave the kiddies up to a million at the regular "transfer tax" rate, so the government hasn't lost anything except a little time. But if you want to leave them more, not only will you pay up to 55 percent, but there will be an extra *grandchild penalty* for delaying the government's funereal intake.

The lesser-known ghouls in this whole operation are the states, who are sharpening their fiscal autopsy tools. Some just take the percentage allotted to it by the IRS, which on $1 million is about 6 percent, credited to your federal account. But other states have assumed a vulture-like position.

Leading among them is Connecticut. Unlike Uncle

Sam, who at least gives you a $600,000 exemption (Mr. Clinton has hinted he wants to cut it back to $200,000!), that state gives you only a $50,000 exemption on your death. That extends the "rich man's" inheritance tax to virtually everyone who dies there and owns even a two-car garage.

That state's inheritance tax rates range from 4.29 percent (who thought up that precise number?) on the first $100,000 taxable, or about $12,000 if someone is left the smallest of houses in lower Connecticut. Heirs might be well prepared to attend the wake with a checkbook. The rate then rises regularly, reaching up to 14.3 percent for relatives and 20.02 percent for others.

Massachusetts has a higher exemption—$500,000—but its rate goes up to 16 percent. With the federal tab, it's really not worth dying there anymore.

Of course, you can try to beat the game by giving your money away while you're alive.

That's not as easy as it seems. The law permits you to give away $10,000 a year to as many people as you want, and not cut into your $600,000 exemption. That means you can give your two children and your three grandchildren, for example, $50,000 a year without paying any tax on it. Your spouse can do the same, which adds up to $100,000.

That's not bad, but consider the pitfalls: (1) You might need the money yourself someday and it will be gone. (2) You could even give away your house to your children a little each year until it's out of your estate. But who knows? They might kick you out when you're old and ship you to a nursing home on Medicaid.

Of course, if you give away more than $10,000 a year to any one person, you have to file a gift tax—the mirror image of the inheritance levy. When Uncle Sam visits you on your deathbed, he doesn't want you estateless and tax free.

The gift tax rates? Naturally, the same as the inheritance tax. The government may be devilish, but when it comes to *intake* it's not stupid, just greedy. (Outgo is a different problem. There they're real stupid.)

Can one beat the death game? Some estate planners think so. They have developed elaborate insurance schemes, which are best for relatively young people for whom policy rates are low.

There's also a whole series of complex trusts that taxpayers should look into. One will help temper the effect of the new Kiddie Tax, which closed the old method of giving away gobs of money to grandchildren. Then there's the Bypass Trust for an aging couple, which may or may not double the $600,000 exemption to $1.2 million.

There's also a Q-Tip trust designed for second wives, who can receive the income from your estate after you die, then pass on the principal to your children after her death. And a Q-DOT trust for spouses who are not U.S. citizens.

There's also a GRAT, GRUT, or personal residence GRIT, which enables a person to give his house to one of his children and yet continue to live in it. When the grantor dies, the house is valued less in figuring the estate—maybe. There's also the Family Limited Partnership, which you must set up before death seems imminent in order to keep the business going and out of the IRS's clutches.

But as one tax consultant, Richard Goodman of Chicago, points out about the FLP, it may be too good to last. "It is reasonable to assume that the Internal Revenue Service will not be far behind in attempting to find a way to diminish, if not eliminate, this valuable estate planning strategy," he says, a reference to the continuing war between CPAs and the IRS.

But of all the schemes to outwit Father IRS, the genius of them all is the Charitable Remainder Trust, a gem which permits you to give away your money and *almost* take it to the grave with you!

According to trust experts, the ingenious scheme works like this:

You donate an appreciated asset—say, securities you bought for $50,000 twenty years—ago that's now worth $200,000. You give it to a charitable trust that you set up. The trust sells the asset for the full price. *You pay no capital gains,* so you're already ahead by 28 percent. The trust then invests the untaxed $200,000 in a mutual fund and gives *you*, while you're alive and kicking, the income directly each year. After you die, the remainder of the trust goes to charity.

And, here's the kicker: You get a partial value of your gift—depending on your age—while you're alive as a charitable deduction on your personal income tax, which can be up to 50 percent of your total income.

What about your heirs?

Well, if you really care, you can use the income from the trust during your lifetime to buy life insurance equal to your gift ($200,000), with them as beneficiaries. On your death, they'll get that money tax free.

There's even a double kicker. Trust pundits say you can set up a family foundation run by your children and grandchildren as the beneficiary of your charitable trust. They can then personally decide where your charity money finally goes. Experts say that your heirs can even draw salaries as foundation officers.

A variation of the Charitable Remainder Trust is the Charitable Lead Trust, which is the reverse of the former. In this case, your donation provides income for charity for a fixed number of years.

What happens when that term is up? *The principal reverts right back to your heirs!* Meanwhile, it's possible to have the full charitable contribution deducted from your estate and escape *all taxes*.

No one less than Jacqueline Kennedy Onassis used the CLT in disposing of what's rumored to be a $200 million estate. It would have been the IRS prize of last year had not the will been arranged wisely by her attorneys.

The will has been described by experts as state of the art. In it, Jackie left her real estate and $250,000 in cash to each of her two children, who had trusts from Onassis set up for them years before. She also left her maids and friends from $25,000 to $250,000 with the added proviso that her estate pay their taxes. But the coup was the Charitable Lead Trust.

The bulk of her estate—superzillions—was given to the C & J Foundation (Carolyn and John, who are trustees, along with Maurice Templesman, Jackie's longtime companion, and her attorney Alexander Forger) over a period of twenty-four years. Each year the foundation gives away a small fortune to charities. *At the end of twenty-four years, it all reverts back to Jackie's grandchildren,* the oldest of whom is Rose Kennedy Schlossberg, who is now seven, and is being groomed to be one of the richest young ladies in America.

Of course, we're not Kennedys. For many of us, especially the reasonably affluent World War II generation, the inheritance tax is a thorn in the side of hard-working Americans who have been mildly successful and want their heirs, not Uncle Sam, to glean the rewards of their labors.

What should we do?

Obviously the inheritance tax should be repealed, as it was in 1802.

It shouldn't be difficult. Once we get rid of the IRS—and I predict that will happen within five years— the inheritance tax will go with it. But why wait that long?

The sooner that happens the sooner we can all die solvent, and in peace.

16

JUNK FOOD TAX

They're Not Looking Out for Your Health

In 1991, the hungry California state legislature, always on the lookout for a quick tax buck, passed what appeared to be an innocent add-on to their sales tax list.

Before that, citizens of the Golden State were able to buy Twinkies, popcorn, pretzels, marshmallows, cheese crackers, and other food tidbits without an extra tab. In that health-conscious state, almost all food was exempt and no one dared suggest that snacks for after-dinner couch potatoes should be taxed.

"Hot food," like ravioli to go from a deli, was taxable, as was food in restaurants served as a meal—where you sat down. Californians tolerated those few intrusions into their gastronomical freedom.

But when a new snack sales tax was passed by the legislature, people became outraged. Nibbles in the car and for kiddies after school would now be more expensive. *Time* magazine headlined the legislative coup à la *Variety*: "TAX WHACKS SNACK PACKS."

The California sales tax is no lite one anyway. The minimum state tax is 7.25 percent, and localties can add on their own. That brings it up to 8.25 percent in Los Angeles, the same as New York City. San Francisco is higher at 8.5 percent, so for accomplished snackers, we're talking real money. But for most people, it was a matter of principle—one more intrusion into the California lifestyle.

Labeling it "The Twinkie Tax," opponents gained national publicity. Since California is an Initiative state (one of twenty-four) where voters have the right to put virtually anything on the ballot, snack lovers organized to fight the powers that be in Sacramento. Children joined in because the law required a sales tax not just on Twinkies and other mushy, sugary baked goods which they love, but on candy as well. Even the revered M&Ms.

Is nothing sacred to the taxmeisters? Apparently not.

One reason why the California law was called a "Twinkie Tax" is that the legislation specifically labeled bakery snacks a "nonfood," a definition that raised the ire of the industry. It also confused the food stores, who could no longer decipher what was and what was not taxable.

Californians of all political ideologies dropped their animosities and got together to protect their sweet tooth. They signed up enough people to put anti-snack-tax Proposition 163 on the ballot, which was no small effort. Citizens of all waistlines went to the polls and upset the plans of the apparently nonsnacking state legislature. In 1992, the law was repealed.

Maryland is now going through the same paroxysms of guilt over taxing what is one of the great luxuries of American life. Their snack tax went into effect in 1992, over opposition, including a warning from Frito Lay, a local company, that they might have to lay off potato chip workers.

"Right now we tax snack foods, what we call 'food for immediate consumption,' " says a Maryland tax official. "It's very complicated. Food bought in a grocery store or supermarket to be eaten at home is exempt, but as the law says, 'POTATO CHIPS, PRETZELS, CORN CHIPS, CHEESE PUFFS AND CURLS, PORK RINDS, POPPED POPCORN (not unpopped kernels, which are tax free), NUTS AND EDIBLE SEEDS ARE TAXABLE.' "

The Maryland opposition reacted so overwhelmingly that a bill for the law's repeal has been offered and is expected to pass.

For some reason, snack taxes seem to raise more ire than much larger taxes. Perhaps it's because the IRS and other taxers are keeping Americans so poor that they have to devour tons of snack foods to assuage their anxiety.

Illinois is another hotbed of snack-tax controversy. There the law is so complex that a tax official had trouble explaining it.

"We have a two-tier system, generally a low rate on

regular food, and a high rate on snacks," an Illinois official in Springfield began. "The low rate is 1 percent and
it applies to most foods, but the high rate is the regular
state rate of 6.25 percent. That goes up to 9 percent in
some localties, like Rosemont, Illinois. The tax applies to
candy, snacks, ice creams, soft drinks, food for immediate
consumption."

It may sound simple that way, but don't be fooled.
The law—86 Illinois Administrative Code, Ch. I, Sec.
130.310—is as turgid as Blackstone's and takes three full
pages, single spaced:

Its interpretations defy a Superior Court:

"Candy bars sold through a vending machine located
outside a service station with no facilities for consumption, would be subject to the low rate of tax, while an
identical candy bar sold through an identical vending machine in a cafeteria, break area, or a location with shared
eating facilities, would be subject to the high rate. . . . It
will be presumed that food sold by vendors with on-
premises consumption facilities will, in fact, be consumed
on premises unless the vendor presents evidence to the
contrary from its books and records."

All this for a little Mars bar.

Junk-food taxes are in vogue. Most of the states that
tax food—twenty in all—tax snacks, as in Idaho, where
they're uniformly taxed at 5 percent. But other states understand that snack taxes can be taxing. New Mexico offers a refund on Twinkie and other food taxes to people
who earn under $10,000, while Wyoming offers a break
to people over sixty-five.

If only we could harness the energy that goes into

such asinine tax rules, or get the lovers of Twinkies on our side. We'd soon have such an army of activists that we could do away with the true villain of the tale—the horrendous income tax.

17

KEOGHs, IRAs, AND 401Ks

They Get It All Back Anyway

Back in 1984, the Smiths, both aged thirty-seven, figured they had it made in the shade.

With their combined income of $65,000 a year, they were able to save a few thousand in the bank. But more important, the government had allowed them to set up the ideal retirement plan. It was called IRA—Individual Retirement Account—and they could each put in $2,000 a year from their salaries, or a total of $4,000 a year.

Most important, the entire $4,000 was tax deductible up front. In their bracket, state and federal, it was really like saving $5,350 a year.

Besides, the money was compounding as they went. All the interest and capital gains—they had it invested in a conservative mutual stock fund—were also nontaxed by Uncle Sam. They did a little arithmetic and figured that if they reinvested all the gains, by the time they retired at age sixty-five not only would they have Social Security, but the IRA would have grown to some $300,000—a cozy nest egg!

But what they didn't figure on was the instability, capriciousness, and fickle nature of Congress and their creation, the madcap IRS Tax Code.

In 1986, in the now-famous (really infamous) Tax Reform Act, the IRA rules were all suddenly changed. It was done without notice right in the midstream of everyone's retirement plans, something you would not expect a reasonable American institution to do. But they did it anyway.

(This constant changing of tax rules—thirty-two times in the last forty-one years—is one of the many reasons Washington has such a poor reputation.)

The new law cut back heavily on IRA plans. The reason? Supposedly to raise money to lower the general tax rates—which, of course, have since gone back up. It also created such a complex jumble of rules that few understood it.

But what the Smiths did understand was that if you earned $40,000 or more, the IRA deduction was reduced to less than $2,000. Then it was phased out completely for anyone who made $50,000 or more. Since their income was $65,000, they were no longer eligible even though they had made elaborate plans for their retirement based on the IRA, including a down payment on a Florida condo.

They were, said their government, "too rich" to be able to continue their retirement plan. In fact, the *majority* of two-paycheck American families have also been cut off from the IRA, proof positive that the middle class is the target and victim of the uncaring federal government.

The government said sorry—you can't invest tax-free anymore. But if you want to put your money in an IRA *after you pay taxes on it* that's okay with us. We'll let the gains ride tax free until you retire. But, they added, you can't touch your own already-taxed money until you're fifty-nine and a half. If you do, you've got to pay the federal government a 10 percent penalty.

Thank you, but no thank you, said the Smiths about Washington's fake generosity. Under that nonplan, the $4,000 IRA savings, instead of being worth $5,350, were now worth about $2,700 after federal and state taxes, or about half as much as before.

So why not go into another popular IRS-approved retirement plan, their accountant said? That's the 401K, which is set up by employers in many cases for their employees. Good idea, Smith commented, but like the majority of small employers in America, the administration of the 401K was just too expensive for his boss, who said "No."

The Smiths were out of luck again. So they went back to the traditional method of saving their own money without the help—or hindrance—of the U.S. government. They would save and sweat out their Social Security check, for which there was also no assurance the untrustworthy government would deliver in the year 2013 when they'd be eligible.

For those who do have a 401K at work, it is a good deal for retirement, and more firms should be encouraged to start one. The way it works is simple.

A 401K plan, named after the tax section that established it, permits an employee to take part of his salary and put it into a plan established by his boss. The employer can add as much as 100 percent of that amount to the employee plan or none at all.

It is tax deductible just as if the employee had not earned the money. (Of course, it does not reduce one's FICA taxes.) The interest, growth, and dividends are not taxable until the employee stops the plan, generally when he leaves or is fired or retires.

That "lump-sum distribution," as it's called, can be taken and taxes paid on it, or it can be "rolled over" into an IRA and protected. The 401K money can't be taken out of the plan before one is fifty-nine and a half, except under "hardship" conditions, which include impending foreclosure of a house, or college tuition for self or a child. If money is taken out prematurely, not only do you pay taxes on it, but there's a 10 percent penalty for using your own money—a big IRS fund-raiser.

Another plan, the Keogh (or HR-10), is highly popular with the self-employed, for it enables them to set up their own "Profit Sharing" and/or "Money Purchase" plans. They can put in up to 20 percent of their self-employed income or $30,000, whichever is less. This can provide a nice nest egg for your old age, but there's one hitch.

The IRS doesn't want you to have all that tax-free money in the bank when you die. They demand that you

start taking the money out of your Keogh a little at a time
once you reach the age of seventy and a half.

Why? Because all "distributions" are immediately
taxable as soon as you get them. Now, finally, clever Uncle Sam is going to get back all the tax money he lost
when you first put it away in your Keogh.

He's also going to get much more. The fund may
have doubled and tripled over the years, and he's getting
the taxes on that as well.

Their theory is that you'll be in a lower tax bracket
at seventy than you were at fifty, and therefore you've
gained. But that may or may not be true.

Meanwhile, thoughts of your Keogh fund growing
each year as you get older and adding to your security after age seventy and a half have been dashed. You *must*
take part of the money out of the plan every year and pay
taxes on it.

How does the IRS calculate the amount you have to
take out? They figure your life expectancy—about sixteen years at age seventy—and force you to distribute
one-sixteenth that first year, then more each year as long
as you live. Instead of your being a rich old geezer as you
had hoped, you'll be getting poorer as you age, feeding
the government with your taxes. If their actuarial scheme
works out perfectly, you'll be flat broke on the day
you die!

And what if, at the age of eighty, as you grieve over
your dwindling Keogh account, you fail to make the distribution, holding on lovingly to the few dollars left in the
plan? That's fine with the IRS.

All they'll do is penalize you 50 percent of the money you didn't take out.

Who says Uncle Sam doesn't have a heart?

18

LICENSE TAXES

The Motor Vehicle Racket

You get on the line at the Department of Motor Vehicles, and wait and wait, and you're finally happy to pay your "fee" for your driver's license or car registration.

The contact is sometimes so painful that the DMV, wherever it is located, is often used to illustrate the psychic dangers of big government.

That much we know. But what we don't know when we pay $25 or $50 to the state is that most of that money has nothing to do with the license. *It's not a fee at all. It's just a plain and simple tax.*

How can you say that? Simple, the great majority of your money is *not* used for the care and feeding of your license, your plates, or your registration.

You're the perfect sucker for that tax because you're a captive at the DMV office. Without your licenses, you can't operate in modern society. So, naturally, you'll pay whatever they ask just to get the needed pieces of paper and be on your way.

How much money is involved? A lot more than you think.

Let's take Virginia, for example. The Department of Motor Vehicles takes in a small fortune from licenses and registration. Does it use it all to run the DMV? No way.

"Our revenue from motor vehicle licenses and registration is $377 million," says a spokesman in Richmond.

And the cost of running the DMV?

Here he got a little sheepish. "About $105 million," he finally responded.

The rest is profit, some three-to-one in income over costs—a snappy little business the public knows nothing about.

Connecticut gets the same good deal from their license *tax*. (Not a fee, please!) That state takes in $217 million from drivers and their cars. What does it spend running the DMV? About $60 million—salaries, fringe benefits, and all. Again, three-to-one intake over outgo.

Where does the rest of the money go?

Well, everywhere. Thirteen and a half million goes into the general fund—which is for the pensions of state employees, among other things. The rest of it goes to various funds, including some for highways, the state police, and most for the Department of Transportation and their buses and trains. In fact, the car license and registration money in Connecticut even goes to pay for Metro North, the railroad commuter line from New York City!

The idea of motor vehicle licensing is sound—to know who's driving, whether they're capable of driving, and who owns what car in case of accident, theft, or mayhem.

The license fees started out nationally as a break-even method of paying for the clerical work. But the *taxmeisters* saw their chance, and those days are gone. Now it's a big-money, high-profit business.

Shaking down drivers to pay for the general fund, as most states do, and to pay for everybody else's transportation, is not, by any stretch of the imagination, a license "fee," as they pretend.

How big is the motor vehicle racket nationally?

Using Connecticut and Virginia as a guide, we can estimate it at *$10 billion a year*, a good piece of tax change. And of that, about $7 billion has nothing to do with your licenses.

What to do?

Simple.

1. States should cut the fee by two-thirds and make it self-supporting, as many of the emissions operations already are.

2. Or at least call it by its real name—a "tax"—then hand out a little booklet explaining where your car registration and driver's license money *really* goes.

It'll make swell reading while you're sitting on a hard metal chair in the depressing surroundings of the motor vehicle bureau waiting for your number to be called.

19

MARRIAGE TAX

Wedding Bells Will Cost You—Plenty

America has a double standard.

One involves pious talk about the sanctity of marriage and the role of the nuclear family in maintaining a stable democracy.

Government spokesmen—including the president in his bully pulpit—constantly proclaim that shacking up, nonmarriage, and out-of-wedlock births are a major cause of social unrest, welfare, and dysfunctional society.

Marriage, on the other hand, is supposed to build a potent polity. In fact, Alexis de Tocqueville, the French sage who visited our shores in 1835, gave the institution of American marriage much of the credit for our stable, prospering nation.

So what does the government do to help marriage along?

Nothing. In fact, that would be a blessing.

What they do is penalize the institution, by using the tax laws to do everything possible to encourage nonmarriage and divorce.

Congress has designed an income tax code that dissuades people from settling down into marital bliss, or even into the conventional version of the historic union.

It's commonly called the "Marriage Penalty" or "Marriage Tax." Although there's no specific antimarriage clause in the tax code, its rates on income are so set that it becomes expensive to get married. In effect, the IRS offers a discount for staying single and living together—with or without children.

This tax law makes no sense, serves no purpose, is unfair, is based on no known theory, is evidence of bureaucratic stupidity, and is strongly tinged with immorality. But it brings in gobs of money, which the hungry government always desperately needs.

Let's take a simple example offered by the House Ways and Means Committee, which claims it is now working on the problem. Two single people who earn $40,000 apiece would each pay $6,633 in federal income taxes, or a total of $13,266. (On top of that, each has a FICA tax of $3,060 plus state income tax, plus, plus. . . .)

But if they decided to make their union legal, they'd pay for it in the pocketbook. Together, just their federal income tax bill jumps to $14,551 or $1,285 more than before they were married, a truly unfair levy.

The marriage tax strangely hits both ends of the economic scale the hardest, poor as well as rich.

The generous Mr. Clinton (with Other People's Money) has enormously expanded the Earned Income Tax Credit welfare program, as we've seen. Under the new guidelines, a poor working unmarried couple—each with one child, and each making $10,000—will receive a tax credit of $4,079—or maybe even a check.

But if they decided to become Mr. and Mrs., they would lose almost all their credit, leaving only $359.

Is it worth getting married if your government and your pocketbook says "No"?

Successful couples are penalized even more harshly. Let's take two baby boomers just under forty. A lawyer (the woman) and a marketing executive (the man) are both in the midst of hot careers.

They enjoy skiing and cohabitating together in a Manhattan condo, as do a number of their friends. But no wedding bells so far. Right now, each has a taxable income of $115,000, for a total of $230,000. Being unmarried, they file separately. Each of them avoids the new higher Clinton tax bracket of 36 percent, which begins at $115,001, and happily allows them both to stay at the lower 31 percent level.

BUT, if Miss Jones convinces Mr. Smith (or vice versa) to tie the knot, it'll cost them—plenty.

As a married couple with a combined $230,000 income, they will have $90,000 of their income in the higher 36 percent bracket, instead of the 31 percent when they were still single.

So getting married will cost them an extra $7,000 a year. Or, as they see it, two skiing trips to Aspen, or even a zero-coupon bond for the college education of a child they're thinking about.

Prior to Clinton, their marriage penalty was $2,600 a year. It has almost tripled in the last two years.

But, you might ask, why not just file separately after they were married? Won't that eliminate the marriage tax? No way.

Uncle Sam is way ahead of them. By filing separately when married, each would hit the deadly 36 percent bracket (that's on top of FICA tax) at $70,001 instead of at the $115,001 cut off when they were single.

The maxim: When it comes to taxes, Uncle Sam speaks with forked fiscal tongue. He loves marriage, but makes you pay more for it. You can't win—unless you're anxious to join me in trading in the IRS for a more compatible, friendlier tax partner (see "Conclusion").

The House of Representatives has devised a small repair of the marriage tax. It will cost the Treasury less than $2 billion a year beginning in 1997 but will only put a dent into the huge amount of cash the government is unfairly extorting from married people today.

Even that small repair has little chance of overcoming the next two obstacles: the Senate and the president's veto.

So until something really happens to reform the system, perhaps you should do what Washington apparently wants: stay single or get divorced and save money.

But the whole distinction is of course asinine—to have different IRS rates for different people to begin with. Why is it the government's business whether we get married or not?

Tell me. Where in the Constitution does it say Uncle Sam can play mother-in-law?

20

NANNY TAX

They Want You to File, and File, and . . .

Remember Zöe Baird, the insurance lawyer? The lady with the unlikely name found out that if you don't file your nanny tax you can't become attorney general of the United States.

Remember Kimba Wood, the federal judge? This lady with another unlikely name also found out that if you don't pay your nanny tax, you can't become attorney general of the United States.

Remember William Kennedy III, friend and partner of Hillary Clinton, who came from Little Rock to conquer Washington? He found that not filing his nanny tax cost him his front-line job at the White House, then exile from the Friends of Hillary circle.

These and other victims of Nannygate in the Clinton administration learned that the elusive tax could be the most important criterion for national political success.

But in more ordinary circles, like mine and yours, the nanny tax can be one simple pain. "Nanny," of course, refers to the British equivalent of a governess, since corrupted to mean domestic worker or baby-sitter, or virtually anyone who works around the house. Then it was enlarged to include those who did anything for anyone and could rationally (or illogically) be considered an "employee."

The original law was, of course, idiotic. It required that if anyone's domestic employee earned *a total of $50* in any given quarter (three months), a whole raft of forms including Social Security, Unemployment Insurance, and a W-2 had to be filed. All this bureaucratic nonsense was for workers who made less than $4 a week!

Few paid much attention to such a ridiculous Washington regulation. But now, because of the national scandals, the tax law has been "reformed," as Beltwayites are prone to say.

Congress has passed new rules on the nanny tax, which cover domestic employees including nannies, baby-sitters, housekeepers, yard workers, and general handypersons.

What is the new threshold of money you must pay out before having to play bookkeeper for the IRS? $5,000 or $10,000 a year?

Forget it. If an "employee" gets $1,000 a year, all of $19.23 a week, you're in for it. So the reform has ele-

vated the nanny tax from the idiotic to the prosaically stupid.

Of course, it had been even worse. After that enormous $50 exemption, the employer of a baby-sitter who came to your home every Saturday evening had to file quarterly IRS Form 942, with FICA, Social Security, and Medicare taxes, along with an annual W-2 form. And, should the lucky employee make $1,000 in any quarter, you had to file a FUTA (federal unemployment tax) form 940 and pay the tax at year's end.

Now things are somewhat better, but still potentially dangerous. You don't have to fill out a quarterly return. You can pay the FICA tax and the FUTA tax on your own Form 1040.

One other break: If the employee is under eighteen you don't have to file or pay anything *unless* the person's "principal occupation" is household employment. Being a student under eighteen automatically qualifies them for the exemption.

BUT, the big IRS question still is: Who's an employee, and who's just a self-employed independent contractor? When do you have to file anything with the IRS?

The litmus test is whether they really work for you or are working for themselves. If they're on their own, you're off the hook. A good indice is whether they work for several people and hold themselves out as being available to others by using newspaper ads, business cards, and having several clients. If it's a baby-sitter who works exclusively for you several days every week, you might be in a little trouble.

One way around the nanny tax is to make sure that

whoever works for you doesn't earn the munificent amount of $1,000 in any one year. (Stop around Christmas time with $995.)

If you want to be sure the cleaning person who may put in a day or a half day a week for you is *not* an employee, try to save their cards or advertisements. Check to see if they work elsewhere, which is a good sign as far as paying a nanny tax. Painters and plumbers, and such, are never considered "employees."

But remember, the Internal Revenue Service has been known to be very capricious.

What can we do to outwit Uncle Sam?

If you want to be even surer that a household worker or baby-sitter is not construed by Uncle Sam to be your "employee"—and thus worthy of withholding and mounds of paperwork—a former IRS spokesman gives this advice:

Have them put their John Hancock on this simple statement:

"I AM A SELF-EMPLOYED PERSON. I PAY MY OWN SOCIAL SECURITY AND OTHER REQUIRED TAXES."

Still, you can never be sure. This is especially true if you intend to seek local office, run for Congress, or have your eye on a big job in Washington, one probably just vacated by someone who forgot to pay his own nanny tax.

21

OPTIONS, STOCK, AND BOND TAXES

It's Mouth-Watering for Washington

Trillions of dollars go through the stock exchange clear-inghouses each year, and not only speculators but the government itself drools at the prospect.

What if they just took a *pinch* of that money with a tax on all financial transactions—the growing business of options as well as stocks and bonds? Wouldn't that make Uncle Sam very happy?

By and large, Washington's been afraid to tax the golden goose for fear it would stop laying eggs. But the temptation was overwhelming. If not a real tax, why not a simple "fee"?

After all, the government, through the Securities and Exchange Commission (SEC), does regulate Wall Street.

Why not ask investors to pay part of the government freight?

No one has yet figured out the difference between a "fee" and a "tax," but everyone knows that "fee" sounds better. And maybe the idea of helping defray the cost of a government service *almost* makes sense. But as we'll see, a tax by any other name costs as much, or more.

The SEC has put in a "fee" on the sale of all securities, bonds, and options transactions through any broker you trade with. It sounds quite small—only one cent per each $300. So on the sale of say 1,000 shares of Ford at $30, the cost is $1. That appears as an "SEC FEE" on the sales slips, whether your sale made a profit or suffered a loss.

They also collect $150 each from the nation's 20,000 Investment Advisers, plus a good hunk of each new public offering in America. The exact amount is one-twenty-ninth of one percent. That too sounds small, but if the stock offering for a new biogenic firm was $100 million, the SEC's "fee" would be almost $35,000.

How close do the "fees" come to paying for the whole SEC operation? A quarter of their costs, or perhaps even half?

Guess again. The SEC (they collect it, not the IRS) took in a total of $588 million in 1994 while their entire budget was only $320 million! That's a *profit* of $268 million.

Did the surplus go to beef up the watchdog of Wall Street's operations? Don't be naive. It all went right into the General Fund of the U.S. Treasury—to be squandered as only Washington knows how.

By any definition, that's a tax, not a fee.

In fact, as the SEC budget goes down and the volume of Wall Street goes up, the SEC tax surplus is growing. In 1995, the SEC budget has been reduced to $297 million. The tax income on securities, bonds, and option sales is expected to top $600 million. That's a profit of over $300 million. Not bad for a little "fee."

The potential of this gold mine for imaginative tax writers has not been lost on Washington. (Archimides commented that if he had a large enough lever, he could lift the world.)

What if Wall Street, whose transactions are collectively equal to half the entire Gross Domestic Product, could be really taxed? The flow of billions would be endless.

Bills are regularly put up by salivating congressmen seeking to double, triple, quadruple, quintiple the "fee," figuring the money boys wouldn't miss it. And anyway, who cares about the small investor, the 50 million Americans who would lose part of their profits to the greedy SEC?

In fact, the Commodities Future Trading Commission, which oversees futures trading, has regularly proposed a fee (tax) on each commodities contract. "It's not a dead issue yet," says an CFTC spokesman. "We're looking for $59 million in new user fees, and it's in committee right now."

Some places, like New York State, home of the most important exchanges, decided to cash in on the golden goose. They levied a substantial tax on securities transactions that was ten times larger than the SEC's. But when the exchanges threatened to move from Manhattan across the river to convenient New Jersey, the tax was suddenly lifted.

Local competition like that can sometimes keep taxes down, but there's no escaping the SEC, not even on a stock transaction made on an island in the Bering Sea.

Investors, watch this one closely. Washington has its flinty eye focused right on you.

22

PENALTIES, LIENS, LEVIES, AND SEIZURES

Please Pay Up—Or Else

The statement addressed to Senator David Pryor at a congressional hearing was poignant.

> Dear Mr. Chairman:
> My name is Kay M. Council. I live in High Point, North Carolina. I am 48 years old, and I am a widow. I came home one evening in June 1988 and found the lights on, the house empty and a note from my husband:

> My dearest Kay—
> I have taken my life in order to provide capital for you. The IRS and its liens which have been

154

taken against our property illegally by a runaway agency of our government have dried up all sources of credit for us. So I have made the only decision I can. It's purely a business decision. I hope you can understand that.

> I love you completely,
> Alex
> You will find my body on the north side of the house.

Mr. Council was only forty-nine years of age, yet he was driven to desperation because of his battle with the IRS, which was destroying his life. It began in San Francisco, where the Councils went into a business that failed, then took a write-off of the $70,000 loss on their taxes. When they were audited, the IRS said their accountant was wrong—that they couldn't take the deduction.

They awaited the "deficiency notice," expecting to challenge the IRS in Tax Court, which is their right. But the notice never came. The Councils moved back to North Carolina, their original home, where Alex started a residential home construction business. Suddenly, four months *after* the statute of limitations ran out, they received a tax bill of $183,021, including large penalties and interest charges.

The IRS claimed they had sent a certified letter years before, but refused to show the Councils the post office receipt. The Councils got in touch with a Problem Resolution Officer at the IRS and gave him all the information. But no one ever got back to them, and when they called again, they learned that the people they spoke with were no longer in that office.

Finally, after four years, the IRS produced their mailing receipt. But it was obvious that they had sent the notice to the wrong address—7+ instead of 71 on the Council's street in California.

Of course it had never been delivered. The Councils badgered the IRS to check the post office records as proof of nondelivery, but they were ignored. Finally, when the IRS did check if the Councils ever signed for it, the post office had destroyed its old records.

(Nondelivery of notices, which often trigger negative IRS action despite taxpayer innocence, can be commonplace. According to a General Accounting Office study of the IRS, 450,000 addresses were incorrectly typed into the agency computers in one recent year. As a result, $49 million in notices went to the wrong addresses.)

Meanwhile the penalties, several of the 140 available to the IRS, were adding up for the Councils. By the time the tax lien against all their property was filed, it had grown to $284,718. As a result, his credit dried up, and his business was destroyed. In a fit of depression, he killed himself.

After his death, his widow decided to fight the case in court. The IRS said that since the Councils knew they owed money (which they denied they did), they should have taken the initiative. *The agency said the Councils should have prodded the IRS to act before the statute ran out!*

The federal court laughed at the IRS claim as preposterous and declared that the lien should be vacated. Not only that, the court ruled that the IRS should pay Mrs. Council's legal fees. Declared the judge: Federal law "does not place upon the plaintiffs the burden of hounding the IRS for delivery of a possible notice of deficiency."

He might have added that the Councils did not feel they owed the government anything to begin with. The IRS finally paid $27,900 toward the legal fees, which actually came to almost $70,000.

An interesting sidelight is that despite her victory, Mrs. Council's credit was so badly hurt by the IRS that she couldn't even buy a vacuum cleaner on credit.

Mrs. Council asks: What if she didn't have money to hire attorneys to begin with? "If you're poor," she asked, "what do you do? There's something wrong when the IRS can accuse you of something and assume you're guilty and destroy your life. Aren't you supposed to be innocent until proven guilty?"

The case is not only important because it resulted in a suicide—not the first one prompted by IRS action—but because it shows several fallibilities of the present income tax system.

In a nutshell, it is that the IRS has power and privileges not granted to anyone else in America, including the president. The whole sense of Anglo-Saxon jurisprudence has been turned on its head by the U.S. Congress, which grants outlandish rights to its collection agency, the IRS, often at the expense of its constituents.

In its mandate to collect as much as possible, as quickly as possible, the IRS naturally savors the idea that

it is an *übermenschen* agency, in some ways like the Ge-
stapo and the KGB. Our own FBI has nowhere near the
powers of the IRS.

It has several ways of enforcing its power: charging
enormous *penalties* for not exactly following the IRS
code; *interest* payments for paying late; *levies,* which include taking money out of your bank without your permission or even knowledge, or garnishing your salary;
liens, which attach your property and give the IRS some
claim on it, making it impossible for you to sell or finance it; and the ultimate, the *seizure* of your property for
any number of reasons.

One of its favorite collection weapons is the *penalty*,
because it brings in a fortune for the IRS. In the 1960s,
penalties were not significant. Even by 1980, the total
penalty assessment was only $1.5 billion. But over the
last decade, the IRS began to change its attitude. Instead
of viewing penalties mainly as a deterrent or punishment,
they saw them as an effortless way to raise billions.
Today, 20 million penalty notices go out to taxpayers
each year.

Many of those penalty notices are in error. The General Accounting Office found that in those cases they
reviewed—which involved penalties for negligence or
understated income—one in three contained errors in
penalty determination. In these same cases, the GAO
found that when a second IRS officer reviewed them,
sixty percent of the time they failed to correct the errors.
Three-fourths of all penalties were not adequately explained to the taxpayer.

One common IRS mistake is penalizing taxpayers

for filing late when they actually filed on time. Lately, there seems to be a rash of such suspicious "mistakes." One taxpayer filed properly on the last day of his extension and was surprised to get a letter assessing him a 5 percent penalty for late filing. Fortunately, he had kept his certified mail receipt and had a signed return receipt from the IRS.

(It's always wise to make copies of all checks and send the originals to the IRS by "certified" mail, return receipt requested!)

He complained by mail and after a few months, the penalty was abated.

The next year, he filed again on the last day. *Once again he got the same penalty notice for filing late—a repeat of the same "mistake."* Little wonder that many critics believe the penalty system is as much a method of raising money as it is a way to punish erring taxpayers.

Taxpayers can ask the IRS to "abate," or forgive, the penalty if they have a plausible reason. The IRS sometimes does, but the GAO audit shows that they are a little quick on the gun to begin with. Examining penalties for failure to pay or failure to file that were eventually forgiven, the GAO found that 29 percent of them should never have been assessed in the first place.

IRS penalties exist for everything: filing late, paying late, paying too little, arithmetic errors, an endless list of ways to extract more billions from taxpayers. Penalties don't necessarily mean the taxpayer has done anything illegal, or sinful, or evasive, or nasty. All it means it that the IRS has an enormous series of penalty codes that they can exercise at will, or whim, and pile one on top of another—even if they're wrong.

A businesswoman was assessed a $400 penalty for missing the deadline for filing a partnership return. She filed on April 9 in plenty of time, but the IRS said that she was wrong. They claimed the partnership was on a March 15 fiscal year, and therefore was late.

She explained that they were wrong—that the partnership was on a calendar year. The IRS agent listened to her complaint on the phone, then said: "OK, we'll look into it, but meanwhile send in your $400 penalty."

One particularly noxious penalty, which began in 1992, can run as high as 20 percent of your taxes. That's the penalty for substantially understating income or underpayment attributable to "negligence" or "disregard of rules and regulations." (Note: There are 14,700 pages of them.) These are broad terms which the IRS can interpret strictly—or loosely—depending on how badly they want your money.

One basic problem in penalties, liens, levies, and seizures is that the IRS has become particularly sloppy in its paperwork, the result of excessive human error, lack of concern for the taxpayer, and an obsolete computer system. The IRS itself admits that 21 percent of all 1040 forms entered by clerks into their computers contain some sort of error, about half of which are the fault of the agency.

The General Accounting Office studied the accuracy of IRS correspondence to taxpayers and found that the IRS failed abysmally. Of 718 pieces of IRS correspondence, 31 percent had "critical errors," and 16 percent had additional errors that were "non critical"—a failure rate of almost one in two!

In testimony before a House committee, a CPA lashed out at the IRS's faulty work, especially when spewed out by their computers. "Computer-generated notices should not be legal," he told the congressmen. "The computer has gone bad again just within the last month or so and the last three notices I have received for clients have all been wrong."

The internal chaos of the IRS is one reason for the many errors in handling returns. Shirley Peterson, IRS commissioner under President Bush, has called the current system "an unwieldy, inefficient, ungodly mess."

Her comments come to life when we look at still another General Accounting Office study. This one showed that the agency doesn't even have accurate records of the $800 million in property—such as cars and homes—seized from taxpayers!

One taxpayer reports that IRS sloppiness, combined with threats of liens and levies almost drove him crazy. He had worked for a small firm as an executive and stayed in the same job when his company was bought out by a large conglomerate. He filed his taxes as usual and had nothing further to pay beyond his withholding. Several months later, he was shocked then he received a whopper of an assessment from the IRS. They wanted taxes on twice as much as his salary, plus enormous penalties.

It turned out that the conglomerate had sent in a W-2 for him as well as the one from his original firm. The IRS computer had him earning the same salary twice. Now they wanted the taxes on the "phantom" salary as well. He sent in letters from both companies explaining the duplication, but the IRS would hear nothing of it. They wanted their money, and their enormous penalty, and now!

This went on for months. Finally, the IRS threatened a levy of salary and a lien on his property. The frustrated taxpayer lost all restraint and screamed hysterically on the phone at the agent, which drew the attention of a supervisor. The matter was finally settled, but only after the taxpayer had exhausted his nerves.

The lien against salary and property means that your income may be taken away and your house held in limbo until you pay what the IRS says you owe. In a recent year, the IRS filed 959,000 liens, all without due process of law and without a judgment and without the taxpayer having a day in court. (The IRS regularly turns up its bureaucratic nose at our revered judicial system.)

Another method of gaining "voluntary" compliance with taxes, as the IRS foolishly describes their methods, is the "levy," also done without the court order some innocents believe is necessary—and with a surprise that can be frightening.

In one recent year, 2,585,000 levies were issued, and millions more were regularly threatened.

A Pennsylvania taxpayer told the Senate Finance Subcommittee overseeing the IRS how his trash management business was totally destroyed by the IRS when they presented him with an assessment of $247,000, then took all his assets. Most surprisingly, they even levied his girlfriend's bank account, seizing $22,000 from it to cover his supposed tax liability. They claimed, without proof, that he was diverting assets to her.

"She never even knew about the IRS liens and levies until her checks started bouncing," he told the senators. "She had to borrow money to buy her groceries and make her mortgage payments."

On appeal, the entire IRS case was thrown out by a federal judge as "unreasonable." But the damage was done. He was ruined, and he and his girlfriend spent $75,000 in legal and accounting fees fighting the IRS. Meanwhile, the IRS agent responsible for it all received a raise and a promotion.

One increasingly common problem in levies and liens involves innocent women, and the apparent trouble the IRS has in differentiating them when they file jointly with their husbands. The IRS logs the return by the top Social Security number, which is generally the husband's.

Worth magazine tells the story of a woman who filed with her husband, but the IRS apparently didn't recognize her existence. The couple had originally filed jointly in New York City before moving to Pittsburgh in 1991.

Once there, the Holtsville, New York, office sent her a belated notice saying she never filed her 1984 taxes. They demanded $7,598.12 including a host of penalties and interest, along with threats that she could lose her home, her car, and her wages.

When she provided the IRS with a copy of her "missing" return, they finally relented. She thought the case was closed, but a year later she received another IRS notice in the mail. This time it was from the Philadelphia office, also claiming that she hadn't filed for 1984.

She finally settled that error as well, but now she says that "every time I get a letter that says Internal Revenue Service on it, I cringe."

Tax adviser Bob Kamman, writing in a National Taxpayers Union bulletin, tells the story of IRS errors involving penalties. In one case, the IRS said a woman had not responded to their request to prove that she had two dependent children and therefore qualified for the "head of household" status she claimed on her return.

The reason she hadn't responded to the IRS was because she never received their letter. They wrote to her at an old address and the mail wasn't forwarded. (Sound familiar?) Did the IRS have her actual address? Of course. She had subsequently filed two additional joint returns with her new address and her Social Security number plainly filled in.

In 1993, she sought a refund of $2,200. Instead, she received a notice that she still owed the IRS money from 1988. They had confiscated the refund and, with penalties added on, wanted $1,000 more.

Kamman went through channels at the IRS, but nothing happened. He even contacted the Problem Resolution Officer in the district, but that too was of no avail. Finally, in desperation, he filled out Form 911 (like the police number for HELP), called "Application for a Taxpayer's Assistance to Relieve Hardship," asking for immediate action. He received a call stating that it was the taxpayer's fault that she moved and didn't notify the IRS—even though she filed two tax returns from the new address.

Kamman had a contact in the national officer of the

IRS and let him know all the details. The next day, the person who had turned down the Form 911 called back to say a refund check was on the way.

(The IRS has $54 million in refunds due to 92,200 taxpayers whose addresses they don't have. The money is being held up until these people write in. That's strange considering how easily they find people who owe them money.)

There must be something within the bureaucratic structure of the IRS which resists logic. One has to presume that the attraction of collecting still more money, pleasing first their immediate supervisor, then the district director, then the commissioner, then the Congress, makes results (meaning cash taken in) more important than efficiency, fairness, or reasonability.

A hint of this basic philosophical error, which can turn the IRS into a rogue organization at times, was shown in a recent case from the Buffalo office. Disgusted employees there filed complaints with the IRS inspector general that managers "manipulated" audits so they could get extra merit pay.

The ability to wield excessive power is at the core of our IRS problem. One of their strongest tools is, of course, the "seizure," something that has an enormous financial and emotional cost to the taxpayer.

The IRS wields that ultimate power without any need for due process, a concept which still shocks this author. Following the tax code written by Congress (a covillain with the IRS!) it can proceed without a court order after it makes a determination that the taxpayer owes

them money. The action itself is placed in the hands of
IRS employees, who often decide on their own whether
to seize someone's property or bank account for monies
ostensibly due.

The IRS officially states that specific procedures
must be conformed to, but others scoff. Jack Warren
Wade, a veteran IRS revenue officer, is one who rejects
the agency's official pronouncements as so much propaganda. He has stated:

"While the Commissioner testified to Congress
about how well IRS policy and procedure protects taxpayers' rights, the managers in the field are quietly sub-
verting national office policy by requiring their revenue
officers to follow *their* policy, *their* philosophy of collection, and *their* whims and moods."

Revenue officer group managers, who must approve
a seizure, Wade says, are often more concerned with collecting enough money to ensure a promotion in the IRS
bureaucracy.

"SEIZURE FEVER—CATCH IT!" said a sign on
the door of an IRS office in Los Angeles, a notice put up
by an overzealous manager. The employee with the
week's best seizure rate was given extra time off as a reward, just as the victims were having their lives ruined.

Testifying before Congress, Joseph R. Smith, of Las
Vegas, an eighteen-year veteran of the IRS, blew the
whistle on some of his overzealous colleagues. "I have
sat on many a promotion panel where the first question of
panel members was 'How many seizures have you
made?' "

Whose fault is this denigration of democracy and the violation of the rights of a free people?

Ours, naturally.

As Ross Perot likes to say, "we're the boss." If so, it's time to exercise our rights as heads of the body politic and purge the nation of such a Damocles hanging continually over our heads.

In the last few years, citizens have learned that the federal government is a wastrel and are *beginning* to take action on that through their representatives and at the ballot box.

Now it's time to give equal concern to our rights as free citizens. Through our Congress, we have granted excessive power to the IRS, power which violates all that this nation stands for—power that must be legally returned to the people.

It's time to say goodbye to penalties, interest, liens, levies, seizures, and fear—forever.

23

PERSONAL PROPERTY TAX

"Are You Hiding Any Horses?"

"People who own horses sometimes like to hide them. They're reluctant to pay the tax," the assessor told me.

A tax on horses?

Oh, yes. That friendly animal is taxable in the entire state of Connecticut, part of their "personal property tax" racket.

Only in Connecticut? Maybe on horses, but over forty states and many counties and cities levy these taxes on a cornucopia of non–real estate property in and around your home. On what kind of things? Everything, from computers to pigs.

Horse owners in Connecticut don't parade into the Town Hall to confess their nags, the tax assessor says. Instead, he uses shoe leather, and his nose, to spot them. There is a $1,000 exemption per horse, which should be enough. After all, how much could a simple nag cost?

"A decent horse for riding will cost anywhere from $3,500 to $7,500," says a local stable operator in Greenwich, Connecticut.

Most people don't ride horses anymore, which doesn't bother officials in Connecticut, Virginia, and a few dozen other states. Cars are taxable as well.

You mean the usual state sales tax? No. On a Jeep Cherokee, a favorite in urbane Connecticut, the 6 percent sales tax comes to about $1,500, a nice piece of change, but only a onetime payment.

Then, you mean the registration fee for license plates? No, that's $70 for two years.

What we're talking about is the "personal property tax" on a car, *which has to be paid every year for the privilege of driving your own vehicle,* on which you've already paid sales tax and registration fees.

Obviously, it's not much money. Right?

Wrong. A $25,000 Jeep Cherokee, for example, has a tax bite of some $300 a year in most Connecticut municipalities, and in the hungry city of Bridgeport, it would run about $1,000. The tab is based on market value, so you can only beat the collector by driving an old jalopy.

The car privilege tax in Prince William County, Virginia, is generally higher than Connecticut's. The yearly personal property tariff on a $40,000 Mercedes comes to $1,500 a year. You could pay off a home mortgage with the car tax alone. In Atlanta, Georgia, another high car tax district, a $25,000 car will set you back $1,000 a year.

You pay it as long as you own the car, and if you don't pay the PPT, the government has an easy recourse. Motor vehicle just won't renew your registration.

Some states, like Connecticut and Virginia, collect the money at the local level, but in others, like California, the money comes in through the motor vehicle bureau. There, the annual car tax dwarfs—by ten to one—the registration fee. California's annual car tax is 2 percent of the market value, which goes down 10 percent a year for five years. So a new $20,000 car would cost $400 a year the first year, and—if you still have it—$200 a year after five years.

The car PPT has been in force in Connecticut for some time and was explained away as a small substitute for an income tax, which the state had never had. When the state income tax was instituted in 1991, people assumed the PPT would disappear. But they didn't understand the inner dynamics of the tax racket. Naturally, Connecticut now has both taxes—full steam.

Several states also tax equipment for small home businesses, like computers. How do they know you have it? They sometimes come into your house and look—without a search warrant.

"I use a lot of shoe leather to find people who've just moved into town so we can assess their personal property," says one of the assessors.

Recently, a young man in Fairfield County, Connecticut, was surprised when a tax assessor came to his door to look around.

"She walked through the house," he recounts. "When she came upon the recording equipment in my basement, her eyes lit up." That revelation now costs him several hundred dollars every year for the privilege of ownership, an unusual form of extortion, even for tax-mad America.

There are many such tax dinosaurs. A survey conducted by the Nebraska Department of Revenue shows that the national picture of personal property taxes is one of crazy-quilt chaos.

There is no rhyme of reason for the levies, and the study reads like a Brechtian play.

Kansas taxes personal airplanes but exempts antique ones. Louisiana taxes personal boats but exempts boathouses. Michigan taxes planes, unless they're owned by Indians.

Alabama taxes virtually everything but exempts peanuts, clothing, and family portraits. Arkansas won't tax your pigs. California will tax your built-in stoves, dishwashers, and carpetry.

Georgia, the land of many tourneys, goes after your golf carts. Indiana levies billboards and vending machines but not cars or boats. Nebraska taxes most personal property but exempts guns, cameras, clothes, and jewelry.

Maine exempts musical instruments, cars, and radium for medical purposes and, naturally, snowmobiles. North Carolina will not tax your dog but will tax your refrigerator and stove.

Ohio taxes almost everything, but lets you off the hook for slot machines, greenhouses, and "graveyard monuments." Mississippi taxes barbershop equipment but exempts small theaters.

Montana will tax your water rights but exempt your sewing machine, while Nevada exempts gold and silver but hits medical and law libraries. Oregon taxes private phone lines but exempts fur-bearing animals.

South Carolina taxes cars, motorcycles, airplanes, and motorboats—unless they're owned by veterans. Texas will tax your boats and planes but exempts buffalos, cattle, and cattalo, a mixture of cattle and buffalo.

Vermont, home of a lot of standing timber, taxes it before it's cut, but won't charge you for cars. The state of Washington taxes captive wild animals but exempts rare coins. Wisconsin will tax rowboats but not art galleries, bees, and horse and wagons.

A few states, including Oklahoma, are even after your furniture!

Furniture? That's right. In seventy-three out of seventy-seven counties in Oklahoma, they tax your kitchen table, your television set, the very bed you sleep in—then hand you a bill.

It's figured simply. They take 10 percent of the market value of your house and assume that's the value of your household possessions. If the house is $100,000, they tax you an additional $10,000 for the privilege of living. But you can cheat them. How? By buying a small house and loading it up with expensive furnishings.

But in resort areas in Massachusetts, you can't get away with that. The state exempts household goods— *except in vacation homes,* of which Massachusetts is full, especially in Cape Cod and the Berkshires, the home of the Tanglewood music festival.

In the Cape Cod town of Barnstable, for instance,

residents pay a $14-a-thousand tax every year on the market value of virtually everything in the house—drapes, couches, chairs, stereos, beds, television sets, pictures, you name it. Even washers and dryers are not exempt.

But anything *attached* to the house is exempt. A dishwasher and a microwave might escape taxation, as would a wall-to-wall rug, town authorities say. But an Oriental rug could set you back a costly penny in taxes.

The picture clause is not elastic, so Cape Coders should beware of owning, or displaying, expensive paintings. If you're rich enough to own an Andy Warhol, you're better off leaving it in your Boston apartment, where bureaucratic illogic has decided it's tax free.

Biggest surprise of the day? New York, that Olympic champion of taxation, has no personal property tax!

Others that leave you alone, a little less surprising, are:

North Dakota
Pennsylvania
South Dakota
New Hampshire
Delaware
Hawaii
Illinois
Iowa

The whole idea of a personal property tax sounds awfully un-American, with town government busybodies poking into your possessions. But there it is.

Still, there's good news. Two of the seventy-seven

counties in Oklahoma are thinking of repealing the household furnishings tax, and California has just exempted some handheld power tools!

But what's the real solution?

Simple. Citizens in states that have this idiotic personal property tax should pressure their politicians with letters, faxes, and phone calls to eliminate it. Failing that, they should defeat any politician who won't vote these onerous levies out of existence.

The anti–personal property tax movement should start with Connecticut, which spends more on education than any other state, so it should know better.

And no, I'm not hiding any horses.

24

PERSONAL PROPERTY (INTANGIBLE) TAX

The Before-You-Die Inheritance Tax Racket

We've all gotten used to having our estate carved up when we pass away, Uncle Sam being the main beneficiary of our life's labors. We've accepted that idea as rational although it makes absolutely no sense, as we've seen.

But some states don't want to wait. Instead, they've set up an intangible personal property tax which cuts into your holdings a little each year while you're still living. To describe it most accurately, it is a WEALTH TAX.

This is not a sales or transaction tax on wealth—there are plenty of those. No, this is a tax on money or stocks or bonds or mutual funds just because you own them and the state would like to become your partner without any further ado. And in about a dozen states, they do.

The state of Georgia is an expert at this premature pilfering. In addition to an intangible recording tax, which costs you $600 on a $200,000 mortgage, they even tap your bank account and your stock portfolio. Not once, but every year, like clockwork.

The Georgia "intangible" (though the bite is *very* "tangible") tax is placed annually on your savings, money, cash, checking account, CDs, bonds, debentures, even accounts receivables!

It isn't going to bankrupt you, but it's a pain, and it doesn't sound very legal, or constitutional. But there it is.

Owning stocks and bonds in that state will cost you $1 per $1,000 of your wealth, or $100 a year on $100,000. People have been talking of late that money is obsolete, and Georgia goes along. Having money in the bank, in whatever form, will cost you 10 cents per $1,000. Even "collateral" has a penalty: 25 cents per $1,000.

Does the Georgia taxpayer get any break? Yes, if he buys stock in a Georgia corporation, they let him off the hook. That's called state patriotism.

Each state has separate rules in this area, creating a tax network that's highly eccentric, uneven, and, of course, quite ridiculous.

Florida is a big name in intangible taxes. They do not tax money, in your wallet or under the mattress, but every year they *do* tax your holdings in stocks, bonds, mutual funds, and money market funds. The first $20,000 is on them. But after that there is a one mill ($1 per

$1,000) on any such wealth you own up to $100,000, when their take increases to $2 for each $1,000. An estate-before-you-die of $300,000 costs $600 a year for the privilege of owning it.

Michigan is another important taxer of wealth they can't see but would still like to get their fiscal arms around. The lake state taxes not only stocks, bonds, land sale contracts, mutual funds, and money market funds (not in the bank) but even annuities.

You save all your life to create an estate, but they get their hands on part of it *before* you cash in. Government plans like IRAs, Keoghs, and 401Ks are exempt, but private annuities pay a 3.5 percent tax to Michigan on any interest and dividends they produce, and the same tax is extracted on mutual and money market funds.

But what if it doesn't produce any interest or dividends? That bothers them not at all. They just tax the whole amount of your holdings each year—by $1 per $1,000 of market value, or $100 per $100,000. Only the first $5,000 is exempt for an individual.

The clever part of the Michigan racket is that it's a double-tax scheme. First, they require that you file all your interest, dividends, and capital gains on your regular income tax and pay at a rate of 4.4 percent.

Then, after $5,000, they require you to file your intangible personal property tax of 3.5 percent *on that very same income* on a separate form—a rather blatant double-tax operation. Now we're talking about a yearly 7.9 state tax bite on certain wealth, which is now no longer trivial—or even funny.

"The intangible personal property tax came in in

1939," says a state official, "and they've been talking about doing away with it for sometime. But so far, it's still there."

And to coin a cliché, don't hold your breath.

Taxpayers have contested the double-trouble operation, but they've lost because of a clever, if spurious, Michigan argument.

"It looks like we're taxing the same thing twice, but actually the income from intangibles is taxed on the regular tax form, while the intangible property tax is really a tax on ownership. We only use the interest and dividends as a gauge of what it's worth."

If that sounds like bureaucratic doublethink, you've got it right.

In the tax racket, as we've seen, everything—if you can see it or even if you can't—is fair game for the tax man, especially in those states that are too impatient to wait until you die.

25

QUARTERLY PAYMENTS

An Expensive Guessing Game

The self-employed, as we shall see, are the most perse-
cuted of Americans in the income tax system.

Of course, others have their money taken from them
just as efficiently. Because of the World War II emergency (most tax rackets start with emergencies), the
Ruml plan began pay as you go, which is better translated
as "the IRS prefers your money in their bank, not yours"
as soon as you earn it.

The self-employed can't have anything taken out of
their salaries because they have none. So it's up to them to
make regular payments to the government. After all, Uncle
Sam has to retain his reputation as a wise old fox who
doesn't like the idea of getting his share *after* you earn it.

It's not only the self-employed who are involved. The "estimated tax" also has to be paid by individuals who take in extra money, whether bonuses, commissions, royalties, interest, dividend, or whatever, as long as it's not withheld.

The IRS answer is quarterly estimates and payments. We're talking substantial money. Some 41 million Americans file quarterly, and pay $154 billion, more than a fourth of all individual income taxes paid.

Quarterly payments are a particularly strange instrument because the government asks you to *guess* how much money you're going to make that year. Then you have to figure out the tax and pay a fourth of it every three months. As the year progresses and your income changes, they want you to refigure your taxes. If you don't guess accurately, there are large penalties and interest tacked onto your account.

The old system was bad enough.

Anyone who had more than $500 of tax liability that wasn't withheld had to make QET (Quarterly Estimated Tax) payments four times a year. But taxpayers had some flexibility. It was logically assumed that they couldn't accurately predict their annual earnings so far in advance.

To soften that guessing game, the IRS waived any penalties if your QET payments were equal to either 100 percent of last year's taxes or 90 percent of this year's. Common sense. Nice fellows.

But now the game is getting rougher. In 1992, the IRS passed a new regulation involving quarterly returns that has made the game even more uneven, naturally in favor of the IRS. Under the new law, if you don't guess

*right, it'll cost you plenty. (It'll cost you even more if you
don't have the cash on hand.)*

The IRS no longer settles for 100 percent of last
year's bill. If you've made at least $75,000 in *any* of the
last three years, and this year you've had a good year—
meaning you've earned $40,000 more than last year—
you've got to guess better.

The old rules don't hold. Instead, 90 percent of your
taxes have to be paid by January 15 (not April 15 like
regular people), just two weeks after the year in question
has ended.

Otherwise? The IRS will get angry and stiff you
with a 10 percent annual interest penalty.

The reason they changed the law, says Congress, is
that they needed the money to extend unemployment benefits. They figured they could collect $6 billion more in
a flash from the self-employed, always a source of extra
cash for the IRS (see "Self-Employed Taxes").

So your rapport with your accountant is increasingly
important. You'll have to visit him more often to figure
out your quarterly returns accurately if you want to keep
Uncle Sam off your back.

The American Institute of Certified Public Accountants is not happy about the new IRS rule. They point out
that in a Sub-Chapter S corporation or a partnership, the
information is not usually available every quarter.

"As they [Congress] see it," says an official of the
AICPA, "they get an extra year of revenue. It's terrible
bookkeeping and it's downright phony. But it's how Congress funds extra benefits without actually raising taxes."

Some tax advisers are happy about the extra work

and income. But others tell their clients to forget trying to play the IRS guessing game. Just pay the penalty, they say. It's cheaper in the long run.

But many taxpayers worry. Won't that penalty call me to the attention of the IRS sleuths? Won't it trigger an audit?

"No way," a spokesman for IRS public affairs has stated. "Sure, the burden of proof is on the taxpayer. But then, it always is. We just don't have the resources to audit everyone who ends up owing us a penalty."

We hope he knows what he's talking about. Nobody in his right mind, even if scrupulous on his taxes, wants an audit.

Remember, the IRS laws passed by Congress have reversed the old American axiom of "innocent until proven guilty." With mad government spending, the rush to collect cash has overwhelmed Washington. Americans now are more likely to be seen as sneakily guilty until they prove themselves innocent.

If that thought perturbs you, lean back, relax, and sip a Coke. Think about that glorious day when we'll all say goodbye to Mr. IRS.

26

REAL ESTATE (PROPERTY) TAXES

They Get Us Where We Live

The Cavanaugh family bought a house in the quiet north side of Stamford, Connecticut, a typical American town of 100,000 split between a suburban end and an inner city. It was 1963, and the home was a decent buy at $55,000. The interest rate in those better times was only 5 percent, so the $50,000, thirty-year mortgage cost them only $268 a month. Shades of Utopia.

The house was "reassessed" about every ten years, and by 1981 the taxes went from less than $1,000 to $2,500 a year. Not that Cavanaugh was happy, but considering inflation, it wasn't a bad deal.

Then came the Connecticut real estate boom. By 1993, the house was suddenly worth $350,000, a seven-

fold gain in thirty years. It made the Cavanaughs feel
good, but the "paper profit" wasn't meaningful. They had
no intention of selling or moving. They liked the quiet,
tree-lined street, and their children and grandchildren
lived close by.

That year, in fact, they paid off the mortgage and
had a small "Burn-the-Mortgage Party." They weren't
saving a fortune, but by this time Mr. and Mrs. Cavanaugh were retired and living on a fixed income. Every
dollar helped.

Then the tax bombshell hit. In 1993, Stamford reassessed all the homes—producing a great surprise for
homeowners. The city counted the inflated value of the
house in their new assessment. In addition, commercial
real estate had dropped (courtesy of the supposed Tax Reform Act of 1986), and the residential homes had to make
up for it.

The result was that the assessment on their house
was suddenly tripled. From $2,500, *the Cavanaughs' tax
went up in one day to $7,000!* The rise in their property
taxes was more than they had saved in paying off the
mortgage!

So what, someone might ask? They're so much
richer now with the higher net worth in their home.

Of course that's nonsense. The Cavanaughs are
much poorer—so much so that their children had to chip
in to save the house from the tax collector. The profit was
on paper, and thus imaginary, unless and until they sold.
But the taxes were quite real.

The whole current theory of "assessments" is somewhat distorted. Because a house accelerates in value

doesn't mean that the people who bought it cheaply years ago can afford the new tax rates.

"When the reassessment took place in 1993, the people howled," says the tax assessor for Stamford. "They went through the appeals system and some got relief of a kind. But other people's taxes went up 300 percent and they just couldn't afford it. We've got a billion dollars' worth of lawsuits against us by homeowners."

California was a particular victim to this during their 1970s real estate boom.

In San Francisco, when the old assessor went to jail for taking bribes, he was replaced by a new assessor with a "modern" view. Whenever a property sold at a higher market rate, notices of higher assessments were sent out to everyone in the neighborhood, along with a property tax increase.

Homeowners got so angry that bumper stickers appeared reading: "Bring back the crooked assessor."

The fight over property taxes is age-old. This is the father of taxes, and the easiest to raise and the toughest for taxpayers to fight.

Why? Because unlike the ephemeral nonsense of the federal government, the local scene is more real and pressing. How many police, or firemen, or teachers, or roads should you have? What is the proper tax rate and why does it differ so greatly in so many places?

All of this is fought out, in typical American fashion, on the local scene and focused right where you live—on your house.

That fight has accelerated in recent years as property taxes have become the fastest growing in America. From

1960 to 1970, they went up in a straight line. Then the cry of antitax groups helped level them out, temporarily. But once local politicians learned how to handle the mob, they started to rise again in 1980, then accelerated.

From 1985 to 1995, property taxes in America have gone up some 10 percent a year—two and a half times faster than inflation. Little wonder homeowners are angry.

There are other forms of local revenue, but property taxes pay for 75 percent of running our towns and cities. Naturally, "revenooers" are much concerned about the square footage and land prices of your home.

Why your house? Because the most effective tax collection method is the threat of seizure. They can't put you in jail, but if you don't pay your property tax, they can just take away your home.

As school costs rise (see "School Tax Racket") astronomically, and the number of local government employees and their salaries and pensions explode, and crime, welfare, and state mandates continue to rise, so do our real estate taxes. Today, they're often as large as our contribution to the federal madhouse.

In many high-cost areas like metropolitan New York, $400,000 houses, which are quite common, carry property tax bills in the area of $10,000. Even small ranch houses in Nassau County, Long Island, long hailed as a suburban paradise, carry tax tags of $6,000 a year for a $200,000 house. In Pittsburgh, houses are taxed at 2.47 percent of fair market value each year. A $200,000 home there would carry a tax bill of almost $5,000, which rivals the Northeast.

Americans are in revolt about property taxes, which are the dumping ground of revenue raising. When states cut their income taxes, the burden is often placed on local property taxes to take up the slack. Homeowners groan, but they pay up.

Yet there is a history of a successful taxpayer revolution. It was in California in 1978 and was conducted by Howard Jarvis, a revolt known worldwide as Proposition 13. It was supposedly even the inspiration for the film *Network*, in which a semi-mad news commentator exhorted listeners to lean out their windows and shout "I'm mad as hell, and I'm not going to take it anymore."

The Jarvis movement was absolutely necessary. In the boom of the sixties and seventies, California property taxes skyrocketed as market values rose and towns cashed in on higher assessments. In some cases, taxes were going up 10 percent a month and people were losing their homes to the tax collector. After Prop 13 passed, taxes were restricted to 1 percent per year of the home's market value as of 1975, and are allowed to go up only 2 percent per year. It also amended the state constitution, requiring a two-thirds vote to raise taxes.

Property taxes dropped 57 percent the first year. One home with a bill of $4,000 plummeted to $700. And most important, it saved homeowners from losing their houses to escalating government. Not bad for one revolt.

Prop 13, which is called the "Acquisition System" of assessment, is still heavily debated in California, especially in an argument between older homeowners who are well protected by that law, and newer homeowners who are less protected. But forms of the plan have been adopted elsewhere, including Florida and Michigan.

The pyrotechnics are not as loud outside California, but homeowners are being clobbered everywhere. The problem is so deep that a cottage industry in specialists who fight City Hall to lower home assessments has sprung up. In Mamaroneck, New York, Tax Reductions Plus find that they can lower one in five assessments in that state by presenting your case, on a contingency fee, before town fathers.

With or without professional help, about half of all assessments are lowered when homeowners appeal, say accountants Coopers and Lybrand. The average cut is 10 percent, so it's to your advantage to complain *if* you have a case. The best way is to check the assessments of houses similar to yours in market value, figures available in your Town Hall. Another way is to look in the local newspaper for sales figures of houses of similar worth to yours and see what their taxes are.

What can we do to solve the property tax mess?

We can and should get an equitable assessment system.

But more important we have to deal with the under-lying cause of high property taxes, which is the size and complexity of local government.

We Americans are government crazy. We have 85,000 local units, most of them overlapping and duplicating each other. In fact, homeowners are often dealing with a half dozen jurisdictions at one time, each eating up tax money in administration and salaries.

A property tax bill from a village in Suffolk County,

New York, on Long Island, graphically shows the crazy quilt of government we're paying for.

This family paid $5,149 in property taxes in the 1993–94 year, broken out as follows:

Commack School District	$2,991.42
Commack Library District	299.13
Suffolk County Tax	309.54
Suffolk County Police District	507.21
Town of Huntington	248.02
Highway District	203.88
Garbage District	326.84
Town Lighting District	31.04
Fire Department, Dix Hills	123.98
Water District, East Dix Hills	107.94

This all takes a lot of people to run. The federal government has 2,050,000 personnel, but that's small when compared with state and local employees. That army totals 17.2 million people!

What can we do to control property taxes?

The first thing to remember is that it's all in your hands. Government must express the will of the majority.

The job of each citizen is to mobilize that majority. To reduce our excessive property taxes, we should take the following actions:

1. Institute an assessment system which is fair to both older and newer homeowners.
2. Work for smaller local government by joining or forming an antitax group. Even put up candidates

against the entrenched politicians if you think tax rates are too high.

3. Eliminate 20 percent of all local government employees, not by layoffs but by attrition as they leave, die, or retire.

4. Put a freeze on local government salaries, and reduce pension systems.

5. Work for local and/or state legislation putting a 2 percent per year cap on property taxes.

6. Seek a state constitutional amendment that requires a two-thirds vote of the state legislature for any tax increases.

7. Do the same with the state budget so that the taxes cannot be made up elsewhere to increase revenues.

8. Reduce the cost of education in your town (see "School Tax Racket").

Citizens in states with the Initiative—there are twenty-four of them—should do it on their own, and immediately. Other states should pressure their legislators to accomplish it.

The sad truth is that local government has gotten too big for its bureaucratic britches, and its property taxes are too high for most homeowners to handle.

Citizens in every town have to organize or join an antitax group and first put a freeze on the size of government, then start to roll it back.

Homeownership is the core of our society, and we can't afford to have our property jeopardized by excessive taxes.

As for my own property taxes, I've had my assessment reduced, but it's still much too high. I'm tired of fighting City Hall on that, so I'll pass that mantle on to someone else.

But I will use my pen to work for a stronger taxpayer revolt against destructive local and state bureaucracy until we have responsive and inexpensive government and much lower property taxes.

Wish us both well.

27

SALES TAX

Shop and Save—Maybe

A mass of shoppers line up, figuratively, each morning at the Maine–New Hampshire border, a straight line that ends at Canada.

On one side of the state border, in New Hampshire, there is no sales tax. Those hardy New Englanders are determined to keep their own taxes low (they're the champions) and to attract business from nearby states.

Meanwhile, on the other side of the border, in Maine, there's a 6 percent sales tax. If you lived in Maine, where would you rather shop? You're right, in New Hampshire. And thousands of Mainers do just that every day, bringing back their goodies tax free.

The same thing is true in tax-happy Massachusetts,

where they also cross over to New Hampshire to shop—
and even live.

In Fairfield County, Connecticut, people shop in
nearby New York City all the time. The Big Apple has a
high 8.25 percent sales tax, but even though their local
tax is only 6 percent, Connecticut matrons travel into
Manhattan, just forty-two minutes away, to beat the New
Yorkers at their own game. They shop in fashionable
clothes boutiques and jewelry stores, then send their
booty home by mail, apparently tax free because it's an
out-of-state transaction.

They've just avoided (or evaded, depending on your
definition) about $42 on a $500 round of purchases,
money lost to New York City, or perhaps even $825
saved on a $10,000 diamond ring.

What this illustrates is the chaos and loonytoon
world of sales taxes, one in which states, cities, and
sometimes villages compete ferociously by establishing
different tax rates to both collect taxes and attract—or
repel—business.

Most every state has a different rate, and a list of
items that are taxable. They go from a low of "0" up to
7 percent in Rhode Island and Mississippi. But that
doesn't tell the full story, for in many states, localities are
allowed to levy sales taxes on top of that. In New York,
for example, the state tax is only 4 percent, and Oswego
adds no local levy. But New York City puts 4.25 percent
more on top of that, making it 8.25 percent, the same as
Los Angeles.

Meanwhile consumers use their feet or cars to try to
outwit the tax people. Shoppers in Idaho cross the border

into tax-free Montana; people in Staten Island shop in nearby New Jersey to save a couple of percentage points; people in south Jersey shop in tax-free Delaware. As we've seen, people in Maine and Massachusetts buy in tax-free New Hampshire. Almost everyone around the country sends parcels home without paying local taxes.

Five states out of the fifty—New Hampshire, Delaware, Montana, Oregon, and Alaska—try it another way. Because they have no sales tax at all, they've become the black sheep of the taxers for setting up "unfair competition" to nearby states.

When it comes to sales taxes, everybody's competing, and everyone's avoiding the tax man as much as they can. Meanwhile, the politicians rack their brains for ways to collect money they believe belongs to them. It's important to politicians because sales taxes in the forty-five states bring in some $142 billion a year.

Who's winning that war? So far the taxpayers are losing there. States have been raising sales taxes almost 8 percent per year for the last decade, an equation for disaster.

When it comes to the avoidance battle—taxpayers who buy out of state and by mail order—taxpayers are still ahead. But the politicians are closing in on this last escape valve. The trouble is that Americans who think they're winning the sales tax war are not aware of one salient fact:

They're actually breaking the law, one put in by angry politicians who can't stand the idea of citizens saving a few bucks.

It's an insane law, and like the 55 mph speed limit,

it's very hard to enforce, mainly because it makes no
sense. But it exists and the enforcement gets a little
tighter each year.

What is this nefarious countermeasure created by
frustrated sales tax administrators?

"New Jersey residents shopping elsewhere may be
avoiding our 6 percent sales tax," explains a New Jersey
tax official, "but it's illegal. If they've bought something
out of state and paid less than our 6 percent tax, or none
at all by buying in a nontax state like nearby Delaware,
or mailing something home from another state—they may
not know it, but they still owe the full sales tax to New
Jersey. That's called a USE TAX, because the goods are
actually used here despite where they were bought."

USE TAX? What's that? Breaking the law?

*Do they really mean that the American tradition of
shipping things home without taxes or crossing the borders to shop in areas with lower sales taxes is illegal?*

Who are they kidding?

First, "use taxes," the other side of sales taxes, are
one of the largest controversies in the world of government. They're the hardest to collect, and the tax that an-
gers Americans more than anything else—when they
learn about it!

It's a law that Americans break on a regular basis
because they consider tax shopping a natural right of free
Americans—to buy what they want wherever taxes are
lowest and pay only the applicable local levy. Unfortunately, they're wrong legally, even though their moral
stance might be perfect.

"Most Americans don't even know the 'use tax' exists," says Carl Felsen, director of public affairs for the New York State Department of Taxation. "The use tax is the flip side of sales tax, and exists in every state that has a sales tax—forty-five altogether. *Everyone who lives in those states owes the full sales tax to his home state on whatever they buy wherever they buy it, anywhere in the United States or even anywhere in the world.* In fact, this is true even if they buy the goods in a nontax state."

What? Let me get this straight. You mean that if a resident of Texas buys something in Montana, which is sales tax free, and brings it back home to Dallas, that she owes a "use tax" to Texas for the privilege of wearing her own dress?

Do they really mean that someone from Chicago who's skiing in Montana and buys an Indian necklace has to pay the sales tax to the state of Illinois?

That's exactly right. The use tax is supposed to be paid by every shopper in forty-five states, people who were sure they were saving a few dollars.

Incroyable!

The use tax is a devilish levy. Even if someone paid sales tax in another state—let's say a San Franciscan whose local sales tax is 8.5 percent bought jewelry in a state with a 4 percent tax—legally he would owe California the difference, or 4.5 percent of his purchase!

So far, most taxpayers have been getting away with it, as long as their state doesn't try to catch them.

"In Connecticut, we have a special use tax form for all those people who buy goods tax-free elsewhere and have it mailed to them," says a Connecticut tax official. "It's a pink form, OP-186, and the taxpayers are sup-

posed to report the goods and services they've paid for
out of state, and send in a check."

How are they doing? How many people fill out
OP-186 and pay the tax?

"We're lucky if we get a thousand forms back out of
over a million taxpayers," he admits. "The average person just ignores it."

This, of course, is driving tax people crazy all over
the nation.

The differing sales tax rates in each state give shoppers a fighting chance, but bureaucrats are fighting back.
New Jersey just sent out a use tax form to likely affluent buyers—60,000 doctors, dentists, and lawyers—and
asked them to confess their out-of-state purchases, adding
a little official warning.

"We collected $9.3 million," says a triumphant New
Jersey tax official.

Maine is trying to stem the New Hampshire drain.
They've put a separate line on the state income tax form
asking about out-of-state purchases.

"It's working pretty well. Some people fill it out.
But if they don't, we just fill it in for them and charge
them a small percentage of their income and send them a
bill for it," says a Maine tax official. "We'd like to get a
list of big Maine customers from New Hampshire stores,
but they're not cooperating. They like their competitive
edge just the way it is."

Michigan too is building a defense against aggressive shoppers who'll go anywhere to avoid the sales tax.
The state is bounded by other sales tax states, so they've
banded together to catch evasive shoppers.

"We've formed the Great Lakes State Interstate Sales Compact made up of Indiana, Michigan, Illinois, Minnesota, Ohio, and Wisconsin to collect cross-border sales taxes," says a Michigan official. "Legally, we can't force out-of-state retailers to collect the tax for us, but we've started a voluntary interstate plan and thousands of stores in the Great Lakes area, including Chicago, have signed up.

"If the customer is from out-of-state, they actually collect the use tax for us on behalf of the buyer." She continued, "Some stores don't cooperate, but when they're audited by their own tax people, we can get a list of Michigan customers and go after them."

How has it been working out?

"Well, Wisconsin has dropped out," says the Michigan spokesperson, "but the other states are helping. I'd say that we're collecting about 5 percent of what's due, which is much better than before."

This all sounds a little scary, even a little Kafka-esque, somewhat like a state invasion of personal privacy. But increasingly the technique is being used by states to collect use taxes on the unpaid sales tax.

New York State audits expensive jewelry stores, then sends the list of nontaxed customers to cooperating states so they can collect. The same is true of several reciprocating states looking for canny out-of-state buyers. One taxpayer in New York recently got a surprise use tax bill for jewelry he purchased in Florida and shipped what he thought was sales tax free to his New York home.

(Is there no government decency?)

Of course, purchases made in Europe are exempt from both state taxes and use taxes. Right?

Wrong. Not even items you buy in Nice or the Netherlands are exempt. The ridiculous use tax is due *wherever* you buy anything, as maddening as that sounds.

"We regularly go through the U.S. Customs records looking for big ticket items bought in Paris or London by residents of New York," says Carl Felsen. "Then we go after them to pay the use tax, which is legally due. In one case, we tracked down a woman who bought expensive jewelry in Paris, and made her pay the use tax, which in New York City is 8.25 percent. Along the way we found out she'd been buying antiques there over the years. We figured she owed us $600,000 in back use taxes."

Fortunately, there's one legal obstacle to the money-hungry sales tax people. That's mail-order sales.

When a mail-order house, like Sears, has a "nexus" in virtually every state, they're required to collect sales tax on all orders in each state. But if a mail-order firm doesn't have an office or salespeople in a particular state, they need not collect sales tax from out-of-state customers.

How come?

Well, in the case of *North Dakota* vs. *Quill Corporation*, the state sued the company for sales taxes on goods ordered by North Dakotans. But the Supreme Court ruled that was interstate commerce. Unless Quill had a nexus in North Dakota, which they didn't, Quill didn't have to collect or pay the state's sales taxes.

Only Congress can regulate interstate commerce, the

courts ruled, and so far they've refused to force mail-order firms to collect state sales taxes.

Sales tax, unfortunately, cannot be helped. But the whole idea of the use tax, the flippant side of sales tax, is repugnant to Americans for many reasons:

1. It smacks of a police state.

2. It's a wealth, not a sales, tax. They are not charging you for a transaction, because that wasn't done in your state. Instead, you're being taxed for something you own, for the "use" of your own possessions. Congress should immediately pass legislation prohibiting such taxes.

3. The use tax is probably unconstitutional and should be challenged again. (Supreme Court please notice.) Buying something across state borders is plainly an act of interstate commerce, which can only be regulated by the federal government, not by the states.

4. The cooperation between states in identifying and collecting "use taxes" will make the present differences in sales tax rates meaningless. It's only that difference that keeps them from totally exploiting the consumer and raising them sky high. As an example, New Jersey has lowered its 6 percent sales tax to 3 percent in Salem County because it borders on tax-free Delaware and business has been suffering.

5. If the use tax is ever truly enforced, states will get together regionally to set high sales tax rates everywhere.

Oh, I forgot. To close the state budget deficits caused by welfare and federal mandates, states are stretching to find taxable items normally considered tax free. In New York State, for instance, *electricity* supplied by Con Edison is taxed at the customer end. Every time New Yorkers turn on the television, they're feeding the state government.

Even more potentially devastating is the movement toward putting state sales taxes on "services." New Mexico, Hawaii, and South Dakota are three of the six states that tax more than one hundred different services, and several others are moving in the same direction.

"In general, states are inching their way toward taxing service industries," says a spokesman for the Multistate Tax Commission in Washington.

If that becomes law everywhere, you'll not only be paying sales taxes to your doctor, but there will be new use taxes if you deal with doctors, lawyers, dentists, plumbers, architects, or what have you, out of state.

The prospect is scary.

I surely can't tell you to avoid any tax, as ridiculous and unconstitutional as it may be. We're all law-abiding citizens.

But the truth is that the use tax is not generally enforced for one major reason: Smarter politicians know it's a rip-off, and a violation of both property rights and interstate commerce.

What should we do?

The only decent thing to do is to get rid of use taxes—posthaste—and encourage, not quash, the competition between the states, the last remaining escape from high sales taxes.

Besides, the pols are taking all the fun out of shopping.

28

SCHOOL
TAX RACKET

Can Money Make You Smart?

"MONEY. MONEY. MONEY."

That's the daily cry of the Education Establishment—teachers, administrators, guidance counselors, etc.—who have been extraordinarily successful by becoming the most effective lobby in America, on the national, state, and local scene.

The politically active National Education Association, the nation's largest teachers union, produces the single greatest block of delegates to every Democratic National Convention.

The results of the Establishment lobbying have been expensive for taxpayers as school taxes have skyrocketed in virtually every American town.

In the last thirty-five years the number of public school teachers has gone up *80 percent* while our student body has increased only *20 percent*. We also now have armies of guidance counselors, special education teachers, and administrators. In affluent Greenwich, Connecticut, there is one full-time professional for every nine children!

What about underpaid teachers, you might ask?

Hardly anymore. In fact, the situation is often the opposite. Teacher salaries have zoomed up 50 percent more than inflation in that same period and now average some $37,000 a year. More important, in the "richer" (read "higher tax") states such as New York and New Jersey, the average is approaching $50,000. That magic figure has been exceeded in the state of Connecticut, and is even higher in many suburban communities. White Plains, New York, pays its teachers an average of $60,000 a year for 180 days of instruction, plus benefits and pensions galore.

But surely all this money and teaching personnel has paid off in a superb education for our children. Right?

Absolutely, totally wrong. Educational statistics not only show that performance is lower today than a generation ago, but that there's absolutely no correlation between money spent, school taxes raised, and performance by the schools.

In 1995, we will spend $6,500 per child nationally, yet those states with the smallest outlays for schools often produce the best results, and vice versa. Utah, for example, which spent only $3,128 per child in 1993, scored

fourth highest in the nation in the SAT (Scholastic Apti-
tude Test) scores.

*In fact, the top ten states in SAT performance—
Iowa, North Dakota, South Dakota, Minnesota, Utah,
Kansas, Nebraska, Illinois, Missouri, and Tennessee—
collectively spent 20 percent less than the national
average!*

Catholic parochial schools, which operate on relatively miniscule budgets, score better on all measure-
ments, from the percentage of students graduating high
school, to college admission, to SAT and other objective
test scores.

*Ironically, the top three spenders in the United
States—New Jersey, Alaska, and Connecticut—are in the
bottom third (#s 33, 35, 36) in SAT scores!*

Internationally, of course, America often occupies
the near-cellar. In one math Olympiad, in which hundreds
of thousands of high school students chosen at random
were tested, South Korea came out first.

How about the United States? Our youngsters scored
fourteenth out of fifteen in math, beating out only
Portugal.

Despite poor all-around results, the cost of education
has been zooming, as have school taxes. The state of
New Jersey spends over $10,000 per pupil as does the
mainly minority District of Columbia and the affluent
suburb of Bloomfield Hills, Michigan. White Plains, New
York, spends $13,000 per pupil—the cost of a good pri-
vate boarding school—a figure topped by several school
districts in nearby New York and New Jersey.

One of the reasons is rising personnel costs. Teachers can collective bargain, but as public employees, they can generally be fired if they strike. (Remember President Reagan's wholesale firing of airtraffic controllers?)

But what many states and school districts do is submit to binding arbitration, which has helped line teacher pockets. Governor Rowland of Connecticut has asked that binding arbitration be discontinued just on health and other benefits, which is raising a howl in the Education Establishment.

So why do we keep paying such a high price for poor education? And where does the money come from?

First, the money—some $275 billion for K-12 schooling—is taken out of every family's fiscal hide, mainly through our local taxes. (The federal government picks up only 6 percent of the tab, most of which is wasted.)

Sometimes the town education budget is a semi-hidden part of the tax bill. Other times, it's tagged directly as "school taxes." In the case of the Dix Hills family we looked at in the Property Tax chapter, the school tax took $2,991.42 of the $5,149 total, or almost 60 percent.

Constitutionally, education is a state function, but by American tradition, it's been locally run and financed mainly by property taxes. On average, schools take 42 percent of those levies, but in areas where education is expensive, the percentage of property taxes used for schooling rises to 55, 60, even 65 percent.

It's a strange tax system, one which originated in 1640 when children were aplenty and farmland was the major asset of the populace. Today, most people have no children in the schools at any one time, and many older houses with high assessments under the new "reevaluation" system, are owned by people with lower incomes.

Teachers and the burgeoning ranks of school administrators have learned the trick of extorting fortunes out of homeowners for their expanded ranks and higher salaries, ostensibly in the name of better education—one of the giant myths of our civilization.

The antitax revolts often focus on school taxes because in many communities, residents have the right to pass or veto the education budget. Unfortunately, these revolts often fail. Parents are uninformed and most citizens are not active in school affairs.

But one recent revolt against rising school taxes has paved the way for a true revolution—one that may be the hope for hard-pressed homeowners.

Little Kalkaska, Michigan, was tired of constant rises in school costs they couldn't afford. In 1993, they repeatedly voted down the school budget, which finally closed down the schools. This set up a statewide debate on how to finance schools, especially in districts like Kalkaska, which didn't have the wherewithal.

To everyone's surprise, state legislator Debbie Stabenow, a Democrat and good friend of the Michigan Education Association, the state's teachers union, proposed eliminating the property tax as the core of school financing, something the MEA opposed.

She successfully argued that the local tax on homes made for unequal school financing. Governor Engler, a Republican, agreed. In 1994, the governor officially abolished the property tax as a source of school financing, cutting out $6 billion in local school levies.

How did they decide to pay for schooling in Michigan?

Today, school taxes have disappeared in Michigan. It pays for schools with an extra 2 percent sales tax and a 75-cent tax on cigarettes.

Naturally, other states are looking at doing the same, which will relieve the pressing property tax burden. At the same time, it will somewhat equalize the amount of money going to poorer districts, which has been the court's decision in several lawsuits.

Both the poor and the middle-class towns seem to win from Michigan's plan. But to some, total state support of schools raises the ugly specter of the loss of local control, a central theme in American culture. This can be a problem, but proper legislation—from the state legislators or by voter Initiative in twenty-four states—can create the best of both worlds: continued strong local control and much lower school taxes, or even none.

This revolutionary era, in which we have the politicians confused and off-guard, is the time to strike.

A good program for those who want to reduce their school tax bill is simple:

1. Cut out 20 percent of administrators in the system. Almost all of the nation's 15,000 school districts are top-heavy.

2. Increase the pupil-teacher ratio by 10 percent. (It seems that class size is not related to quality teaching. In Seoul, South Korea, there are fifty-five children in the average class, and American classes were much larger when our education was better!)

3. Set a cap on rising school costs, tying them to a third less than inflation.

4. Eliminate all binding arbitration in school pay disputes and rely on collective bargaining. Binding arbitration has been a major cause of rising school district taxes.

5. Rethink teacher and administrator pension policy. The plans are generally much too rich.

6. Raise the retirement age of teachers. Many retire at fifty-five or less.

7. Make the school tax a fixed, lower percentage of your town's budget. If it is over 50 percent, reduce it to that level.

We all have to be concerned about poor public school performance. It's a national disgrace, especially since we are supporting an enormous professional staff with excessive school taxes.

But it's important not to connect cost cutting in our school budgets with any loss of learning for our children. As we've seen in so many cases, including parochial schools, money is not related to the quality of education.

That's a factor of better curriculum, more rigorous instruction, and the dedication of students and faculty—a truth borne out by virtually every standardized test score.

The Establishment's cry for more money and the threat that smaller school budgets will hurt our children is just the propaganda siren song of the education special interest group.

What can the average citizen do?

Don't just complain about school district taxes. Get in there, become active in educational affairs, even run for the school board. Help cut down the costs and raise the standards. And perhaps follow Michigan's path and just get rid of the school taxes entirely.

It's your choice, and challenge.

29

SELF-EMPLOYED TAXES

Double Trouble

Fed up with your boss?

Ready to follow the American dream and go out on your own—doctor, lawyer, Indian chief?

Better think twice before you leap. Uncle Sam and the IRS have you targeted.

Today, the self-employed American is more likely to be an architect, carpenter, photographer, insurance agent, writer, money manager, publicist, and operator of millions of mom-and-pop operations.

Isn't that what America's all about: ingenuity and freedom?

So the propaganda goes. But the reality is quite the opposite. Uncle Sam and his local allies do everything possible to make life miserable for those who strike out on their own. If you follow your own star be ready to suffer special tax bites you never dreamed of in this galaxy.

Doesn't this involve an insignificant number of Americans?

No more. Actually, self-employment is the quickest-growing part of the American workforce. A new self-employed worker takes that first step every sixteen seconds, according to the Small Business Survival Committee. Sometimes it's because they want the freedom. Often it's because they've just been laid off in a corporate downsizing that has put 350,000 people on the street in 1994 alone. Or they might be one of the 1.2 million who've lost good paying jobs in manufacturing in the last five years.

With no similar jobs available, only the challenging world of self-employment awaits many.

Estimates of the number of self-employed vary anywhere from 14 to 33 million depending on the definition. But in any case, it involves a large slice of the American workforce, and is growing rapidly.

What does Uncle Sam do to help them?

Nothing. In fact, quite the opposite. The biggest shock takes place when they learn about their new, much larger, FICA (Social Security, Medicare) tax. As employees, they had 7.65 percent of their income taken out, and their employer paid an equal amount, a total of 15.3 percent. But as self-employed they must pay nearly *double* FICA taxes.

And as Americans already know, these taxes, unlike

state and property taxes, are not deductible from the income tax bill.

Do they get extra benefits when they retire, a kind of bonus for the extra FICA taxes paid in over the years? You must be kidding.

The men who developed the mad concept that one person is actually two (double trouble) were of course well-employed by the government, even if some were intellectually deficient. They set up a system where both the employer's contribution of 7.65 and the employee's contribution of 7.65 had to be paid by the self-employed, putting an onerous burden on the most vulnerable people in our society.

And unlike the myth of riches, most self-employed are just scrounging out a living, averaging only $18,000 annually—$7,000 less than employed Americans. (These figures even include our super-wealthy doctors and lawyers.)

As a partial sign of remorse, Congress gave them a small break in 1990 by allowing a tax deduction—but not a tax *credit*—of half the amount, which typically reduces the 15.3 percent to an equally intolerable 13.2 percent of their income.

Let's take a self-employed photographer who makes $40,000. His FICA tax alone is $5,400, which with federal income taxes, state income taxes, property taxes, sales taxes, is too much for anyone. He can't deduct the sales taxes, nor can he deduct his FICA taxes. The plain truth is that he just can't afford to live decently.

Now, let's look at another self-employed person, an architect, who makes $61,200 a year, the present upper limit for FICA taxes. That number times 13.2 percent means that this person pays $8,079 in FICA tax annually. In his regular income tax, he's in the 28 percent bracket. Adding his FICA "contribution," as the government laughingly calls it, his marginal tax is now 41.2 percent, an impossible burden that can reach to the 50 percent level when other taxes are thrown in.

That extra FICA tax puts him over the top in anxiety and debt, to which the self-employed are overly subject. It also makes him poorer than his employee neighbor next door with the same income. That's not nice.

Now let's say our self-employed person—doctor, lawyer, financial adviser—makes $100,000 a year (God bless him). How much will he pay in self-employed tax? Is the $61,200 limit, which goes up each year (a secret tax increase not mentioned by politicians), the top-top?

Lots of luck. Congress and the president, in their infinite indifference, have lifted the Medicare part of the FICA tax all the way up with no limit. To an employee who makes $100,000 this adds an extra $550 to his FICA tax. But to the self-employed, it raises it almost $1,000. This makes his self-employed, nondeductible FICA tax almost $10,000 a year.

The self-employed person of any age actually pays even more into Medicare than it appears. The new "Medicare" self-employment tax is not levied on the gross adjusted income, or even on the "taxable income." It comes off the very top and does not allow for such deductions as *mortgage interest, property tax, state taxes, or anything else* that's allowed on regular income tax.

Nor does it allow a deduction for the Keogh self-employment retirement plan. Instead of an extra 2.9 percent for Medicare, it really is more like a 4 percent jump in income tax for the self-employed, on top of the extra 6 percent on the FICA amount. No wonder more Americans are paying more in FICA these days than the other, or regular, income tax!

And self-employed people are penalized another way—in atrocious penalties and interest for not keeping up with their quarterly withholdings. Just talk to a self-employed person who gets paid *irregularly* but must pay the IRS *regularly.* His mutterings may sound like treason, but it's just the steam from Americans made fiscally insane by a punishing tax system.

No one doubts that the self-employed person's income goes up and down much more than other taxpayers. But not only doesn't Uncle Sam care, he gloats. In 1986, in the so-called Reform law, he took away Income Tax Averaging, which used to even out things a little.

No more. If the self-employed person makes nothing one year and $100,000 the next, he pays on the full $100,000—even though he may have to use much of it to pay back what he borrowed to live on in the leaner years.

It's just another nail in the coffin of ingenuity, individuality, freedom, and invention, the four things that used to make America great.

Oh, I forgot. When he was laid off and entered the wonderful world of self-employment, our taxpayer lost his group health insurance, which used to cost him little, or nothing.

And now? Many states require organizations like Blue Cross/Blue Shield to cover self-employed people and their families.

But at what cost? Connecticut BC/BS has a plan for just such cases. Cheap? No way. Not for the self-employed. A family policy costs $9,300 a year! And if you want to save, you can join their HMO for *only* $6,300 a year, almost double the premiums of those regularly employed.

Now add that to his self-employed FICA tax, income tax, state income tax, property tax, etc., and what do you have? Independence? More likely *agita.*

If you're lucky enough to be able to afford such a health plan, surely Uncle Sam allows you to deduct the cost of it from your taxes. No way. You could once deduct 25 percent of it, but even that small break expired in 1993 and was only put back into force in the spring of 1995. Even with that small tax deduction, the family health plan will still set you back $8,600 net!

Is that the only onerous burden for the self-employed? No. In New York City and other tax hells there's another hit. It's called the Unincorporated Business Tax for the self-employed, which is levied on everyone from photographers to chiropractors.

What can we do to fix this mess of trying to be self-employed and live in the USA at the same time?

1. Change the law so that the self-employed pay the same as any other American into FICA—a total of 7.65 percent.

2. If the government won't do that, change the whole system so that the self-employed are allowed to "contribute" to FICA on a voluntary basis from year to year, and have their Social Security check reduced accordingly when they retire.

3. If the government still won't budge, allow the self-employed to opt out of the system *entirely* if they want, and set up their own retirement with the money. They'll end up much richer at sixty-five (see "Social Security Taxes").

4. *All* health insurance payments for the self-employed should be deductible from their federal taxes, as was once the case.

Meanwhile, take my advice. Until the self-employed are released from the FICA Follies, maybe you should forget the American dream of independence. Go back and work as a wage slave for Corporation X—until they lay you off.

Then you'll have no choice but to join the army of oppressed individuals who believe they're working for themselves but are *really* toiling mainly for Uncle Sam.

30

SIN TAXES

A Taxing Life

Whenever the government needs money, they think of the sinners—smokers and drinkers—who, the theory goes, will spend any amount of money to maintain their pleasures, and whose pockets Uncle Sam can then pick.

The interesting part of sin taxes is where they reside. They're not in the IRS, but in the Bureau of Alcohol, Tobacco and Firearms in the Department of Treasury, which acquired firearms not long ago from Internal Revenue.

What do these items have in common?

Apparently, they seem nefarious to some, a kind of moral delinquency requiring not just larger taxes but a single agency to monitor them.

How come? Well, we know that cigarettes contribute to cancer, so they belong in the tax leper world.

Whiskey? We still think of the Lost Weekend and AA meetings, even though the American Heart Association says a little alcohol in your diet is good for the heart. Wine, naturally, is de rigueur for a sophisticated dinner or picnic on Big Sur, but too much, doctors warn, is bad for your liver.

And firearms? Visions of Chicago gangland fights of 1929, the Waco showdown, and the use of assault weapons in crime all unite to tie firearms into this triumvirate of nasty behavior, as Washington sees it, tax-wise. (Others, of course, point out that the Second Amendment protects the right to bear arms.)

There is even a fearsome fourth item handled by the ATF. That's explosives. Normally used to build roads, they're also a tool of mad terrorists, like those who blew up the World Trade Center.

So the unifying theory seems to be the potential for mayhem—and therefore justifiably high taxes on all.

How high are the sin taxes?

Pretty high.

Take your usual "fifth" of liquor, which is actually 750 millimeters, or three-quarters of a liter. It's usually 80 proof alcohol, which is the measure used to tax it.

How much? The retail price of a typical bottle comes to $9.22, according to the Distillers Association. Of that, $4.08 is taxes—or some 44 percent. The federal tax is $2.15 per bottle, paid by the distiller or the importer, and secretly built into the price so that the consumer has no idea what he's paying to whom.

The states refuse to be ignored and pulls off the same racket of hidden levies. State taxes on the same bottle of "spirits" (as it's still known) run almost as high, taking $1.92 per bottle. The other $5.14 is divided between the wholesaler and retailer.

The state champion in whiskey taxes is Alabama, which puts a $5.42 tax on the typical bottle! Together with the federal tax, a *total of $7.57 is taxes*, or two-thirds of their state's average retail price of $11.39. That leaves only $3.82 for the actual product, both wholesale and retail.

Other high whiskey tax states are Oregon ($4.30 per bottle) and Michigan ($4.30), and the state of Washington ($4.15). The most lenient on drinkers is, surprisingly, Massachusetts (only 81 cents), Missouri (85 cents), Maryland (89 cents), and Colorado (95 cents). One of the hardest-drinking towns in America, the District of Columbia, charges only $1.08.

"High taxes are one of the things killing our business," says a spokesman for the Distillers Association in Washington. "The rise in taxes in 1992 produced a drop in business of 7.5 percent over 1991. But the government didn't gain anything. They reached the point of diminishing returns and took in $89 million *less* in liquor taxes."

The typical tax on a six-pack of beer, the choice of middle America, is kinder: 33 cents federal plus 44 cents state and local. The champion six-pack taxer is Tennessee with 92 cents on top of the federal, or $1.24 a six-pack, enough to stimulate drunkenness. (Georgia is the runner-up.) Massachusetts, the onetime blue-stocking state, is again the most lenient with drinkers, with only an 8-cent tax. Delaware is a close second.

The higher the alcohol content in whiskey, the higher the taxes. One hundred proof spirits like Smirnoff vodka and Wild Turkey 100 bourbon pay some 20 percent more in taxes to the ATF. But this isn't true of wine, whose federal tax is 22 cents a bottle (along with state levies) regardless of the alcohol content. The big wine taxer is Pennsylvania, which adds $1.52 to each wine bottle. Utah, home of nondrinking Mormons, is the runner-up with a high tax of $1.18.

The lowest tax on wine? Again, it's Massachusetts with only a 12-cent tariff.

There's also a sin tax on people who sell it. These "occupational taxes" are $250 for retail stores and $500 for wholesalers. The ATF even charges dealers in industrial alcohol (you'd better not drink the stuff) a $250 fee.

How much do governments collect from all nippers?

A total of $17 billion, divided $7.7 billion for Washington and $9.5 billion by the states and localities. To that add a sales tax of about 60 cents on a $10 bottle. That's mainly a tax on a tax, since half the price of the bottle is a levy to begin with. (That's not nice, and probably unconstitutional, but there it is.)

Cigarettes don't have alcohol's American Heart Association imprimatur, but they bring in a fortune for the tax collectors as well.

The federal tab was $5.7 billion in 1994, plus $6.4 billion from the states, and going up rapidly. States keep hiking the tax in the name of health, but they keep the sinful money anyway. In addition, there are proposals afoot in Congress and the White House to raise the tax on cigarettes anywhere from 25 cents to $2.00 a pack.

Overall, the tobacco tax take (they also tax snuff, pipe tobacco, cigars, and chewing tobacco) is close to $13 billion a year, which will surely double before the turn of the century. Unless, of course, the high taxes cut down the usage and backfire on the taxers as is happening with whiskey.

What's the present tax on cigarettes? Actually, the federal tax is lower than that of most states. A 20-pack is taxed 24 cents by Washington, on top of which the states add anything from 81.5 cents in Washington State (effective July 1, 1995) to 65 cents in high-stress D.C. to 60 cents in Hawaii, 58 cents in Arizona, 56 cents in New York and Rhode Island, 51 cents in Massachusetts, and 50 cents in Connecticut.

Where are cigarettes taxes the lowest?

Guess. Naturally in the tobacco raising states: a mere 2.5 cents per pack in Virginia; 3 cents in Kentucky and 5 cents in North Carolina—the core reason for the cigarette smuggling from those states to the high-tax Northeast.

And again, like whiskey, cigarettes are double-taxed by states and municipalities through their sales taxes—a tax on a tax. (And don't forget: if you buy them out of state, you owe your local "use" tax.)

New York City, like many municipalities, puts its own tax on top of the federal and state. In this case, it's an 8 cents a pack surcharge. That tax, says a Tax Foundation study, cuts into New York's sales through both cross-border sales—people buying their cigarettes in low-tax Virginia or actually smuggling them in from Kentucky, North Carolina, and Virginia.

The result of the super-tax? The Big Apple, says the Tax Foundation, loses $239 million in sales each year!

When it comes to taxes, smokers had better watch out, particularly since that's one tax that nonsmokers like.

The third leg of the ATF operation is firearms, which we'll briefly explore in the Excise Tax chapter. They bring in a relatively small amount, only $170 million, broken up into various tax categories, from pistols and revolvers, 10 percent; to other firearms like rifles, 11 percent; and shells and cartridges 11 percent. (Bows and arrows, 11 percent, were left with the IRS as a concession.)

Firearm dealers, of whom there are many, pay a $10-a-year license fee. But for some reason, *pawnbrokers* are soaked more ($25) just to handle a few guns. Explosives make up the fourth leg of the ATF operation, and these are what they refer to as "Destructive Devices." There, the dealer who handles them pays a fee of $1,000 a year.

But when we talk about sin taxes, the big action is in whiskey, wine, beer, and cigarettes. These habits, or pleasures, cost Americans a lot of money—some $30 billion a year. Surely, as an avuncular figure, Uncle Sam gets despondent when he thinks about his people smoking and drinking so much.

On the other hand, when he looks at the bottom line, the old man must really smile.

31

SMALL BUSINESS TAXES

How to Kill the Economy

Every politician claims to love small business. You hear it every day:

"Small business is the heart of American enterprise."

"Small business is the largest employer in America."

"Small business is the future of this country."

The rhetoric is magnificent, but the reality is perverse. The greatest enemy of small business is not local or global competition, but American governments and their tax policies, from Washington to the hometowns.

Small business accounts for 48 million workers, 8 million more than big business, says the National Federation of Independent Business. Dun & Bradstreet adds

that these plucky entrepreneurs are responsible for eight
out of every ten new jobs created in the nation.

Small business is the fastest-growing element of our
society, and it doesn't take a Ph.D. in economics to understand that it represents the future. This is truer today
than ever, especially since big business is constantly "re-
structuring" and laying off people to enhance their bottom line and stock price.

One of the fastest of the fastest, says the Small Business Survival Committee, is the self-employed home-
based workforce, which has tripled since 1980 (see
"Self-Employed Taxes"). Some small businesses take in
over a million dollars annually, but the majority, says the
SBSC, have between only one and four employees. Here
small really means small.

The problem is that despite their importance, small
business has become the target of tax-mad politicians.
Big business takes care of itself by hiring lawyers and
raising prices when all else fails. But all that keeps many
small firms from going under is American ingenuity, the
sixty-hour workweek, and their stubborn defiance against
the crippling political Establishment.

Take a copy-printing shop in Connecticut, a small
operation that employs three people. The proprietor rat-
tled off the taxes he has to pay, along with the painful
and time-consuming paperwork headache.

The litany of taxes seems endless:

1. Monthly deduction of withholding of federal taxes
for the owner and three employees—sent monthly to a local bank which deposits it to the federal government.

2. Deduction of employee's FICA taxes, which rep-

resents 7.65 of the payroll (from the top and not after withholding), mailed to the government monthly.

3. The employer's contribution of 7.65 of the payroll for FICA, also mailed to the federal government monthly.

4. Withholding of state income tax of 4 percent for employees, sent to the state monthly.

5. Workers' Compensation, required by state law, and fully paid for by the employer. The rate depends on the firm's accident and health experience.

6. Personal property tax, which is not at all personal. It's a continuing yearly tax on all his business equipment and supplies, including printing presses, computers, copying machines, desks and calculators, furniture, even supplies of blank paper. Set up by state law, this strange tax is paid to the town at the same rate as real estate.

That tax is particularly stupid since it is a disincentive to buy new equipment and expand.

7. State unemployment insurance for his employees, figured at a percentage of the payroll, from 2 to 6.9 percent, depending on the unemployment history of the firm. The business pays that in full; the employee contributes nothing.

8. Federal unemployment insurance (FUTA), also paid in full by the business.

9. Sales tax. In addition to acting as a collection agent for the state tax (6 percent), he pays this on all equipment and supply purchases. Only paper, which is "resold," is exempt.

10. Use tax on all supplies he buys outside the state and has shipped to him.

11. State corporate income tax. His is a Sub-Chapter "S" so the profits flow through personally to him. But he has a yearly minimum corporate tax, and biannual filing fees with the secretary of state, plus accounting fees. Small businesses which are regular "C" corporations pay a federal corporate income tax of up to 34 percent, plus a state corporate income tax.

12. He rents so he doesn't have a real estate tax, but millions of small businesses do. They also have a property tax on the land and office, or factory, in which they do business. In fact, several localities charge business a "commercial rent tax" whether they own the property or not.

13. He's lucky that he doesn't have to pay a gross receipts tax, which is common in many localities, and comes right off the top. For noncorporations, many areas, such as New York City, have an Unincorporated Business Tax.

Enough? Yes, quite.

How are small businesses doing?

The business economy is not bad, but they still must fight for survival. *The tax burden is onerous and getting worse every day.* A survey done for the Small Business Survival Committee shows the negative effect of just the federal tax increase of 1993.

Almost 70 percent responded defensively. More than a fourth raised prices, another fourth postponed expansion plans, one in seven fired at least one employee, and 9 percent took two of the actions.

The survey also asked small business people whether they thought the government was a partner or an opponent in their pursuit of the American dream?

Fifty-nine percent answered "opponent." Only 32
percent saw government as an ally. The most surprising
result was that the *employees* were angrier than their
bosses. Sixty-three percent of them considered the government an enemy!

A big blow against small business in the 1993 tax
hike involved the hundreds of thousands of those which
are run as "S" corporations, like our print shop in Connecticut. By a strange twist of the new tax law, some
were forced into a higher tax bracket than IBM!

How come? Because regular corporations have a top
tax rate of 34 percent. But "S" corporations, which tend
to be small one-owner operations, pay as if they are individuals, whose new top rate goes up to 42 percent!

Not all small businesses shoulder the same burden.
Taxes vary enormously by location. The National Feder-
ation of Independent Business did a survey of tax costs
for five theoretical small businesses in forty-four cities.
They ranged from Bigg Manufacturing, which grossed
$23 million a year, to a small janitorial service (Clean
Sweep Maintenance), which took in only $300,000.

They didn't include income tax withheld, or even
FICA taxes paid by the employees. Nor did they include
Workers' Compensation, even though it's required by law
in all but three states. But they catalogued all the usual
taxes.

Which towns punish small businesses the most?
They found that the worst tax city was Seattle, fol-

lowed by New York City, then by Portland, Oregon, and, most surprising, by Columbia, South Carolina.

Who were the winners—meaning the towns with the lowest tax burden?

That was a runaway for two frugal cities: Manchester, New Hampshire, and Austin, Texas. The runner-ups were Houston, Texas; Montgomery, Alabama; and Springfield, Illinois.

Also gnawing at small businesses nationwide is federal regulation, a form of hidden taxes. Business was once underregulated and workers had little protection from environmental hazards and accidents. Today, the situation is reversed. Big business can hire lawyers and fight OSHA (Occupational Safety and Health Administration), but small businesses are strangled by their demands.

OSHA helped make the workplace safer, but—like much in Washington—it can go overboard with asinine bureaucratic rules. Recently, they fined a California dry-cleaning firm $250 for not posting the number of workers who had been injured on the job during the last year. The only trouble was that no one was injured, so there was nothing to post.

Workers' Compensation, a necessary idea to protect workers, has been so abused that it's crippling many small companies. WC started out as a no-fault operation, but somebody forgot to tell the lawyers. Today, one large judgment from an award-happy jury can triple the insurance rate of a small company.

Forty-seven states require WC, so it's really a tax. Over the last decade it's been a disaster, premiums rising at the rate of over 10 percent a year in three recent years, to the point where it's now a $70 billion nut for business.

Regulation is a *bête noir* for small business. It's now supposedly being lessened (perhaps) by the 104th Congress, but the cost to small business is still horrendous. Just in 1994, Washington, not counting the states, added 67,927 pages of notices, proposed rules, and final regs to the Federal Register. From 1989 to 1992, says the Joint Economic Committee of Congress, the regulatory burden on small business rose 34 percent to a cost of $130 billion!

Maybe IBM can handle that kind of chaff, but Mom and Pop's Shoe Store, or Mike's Chewy Pizza Parlor, surely can't.

Is it only small businessmen complaining about Uncle Sam?

No way. A study of employees of small firms showed that 70 percent of them believe that "there are too many workplace regulations."

Then what should you do if you want to go into business for yourself?

First, realize that you've got Washington, your statehouse, and your town armed against you. But if you're insistent, just hold your nose and open your doors.

The best advice I can give is to move to Austin, Texas. It happens to be a nice town, and you'll feel the heavy hand of government taxes just a little lighter on your back.

32

SOCIAL SECURITY TAX

Pay Now; Get Ponzied Later

In 1982, Washington pundits headed by Senator Daniel Patrick Moynihan of New York and Alan Greenspan, now chairman of the Federal Reserve system, met to handle a crisis.

The Social Security system was in danger. The great scheme started by FDR as the Old Age and Survivors Insurance Act of 1935 was ostensibly going belly-up.

The idea was frightening, as it should be. Of course, there was enough money coming in from the FICA (Federal Insurance Contributions Act) taxes to meet the claims of seniors on Social Security—now 36 million strong. But the system was future-broke.

By the year 2020, maybe even the year 2015, the

committee calculated, there wouldn't be enough money in the kitty to handle the baby boomers, who would be starting to retire in enormous numbers.

What to do to "save" the Social Security system?

The answer seemed simple. Raise the FICA taxes almost 25 percent to 15.3 percent of all payrolls, bringing in more money than the world has ever seen—over $400 billion a year today. The idea was to generate a giant surplus beginning in 1983, then squirrel it away for the baby boomers. They would need at least *$2 trillion* for Social Security to stay solvent in the twenty-first century.

Has the scheme worked?

No. In fact, it's been an unmitigated disaster.

The only part of the scheme that works is that the raised FICA taxes bring in gobs more money for the wastrel government. The FICA tax receipts are now so enormous that the median income American family paid more in FICA taxes in 1994 than they did in straight income taxes!

(The best way to look at it is this: There are really two federal income taxes. One of them is masquerading as a pension plan.)

In fact, the Social Security tax has been bringing in so much money that the desperate deficit-ridden government was tempted. Why squirrel away cash for the future if they could use the surplus from the tax increase right now? They yielded, and the scheme, like so much dreamed up by Washington, has become both a fiscal failure and a prime example of philosophical corruption.

The plan for the twenty-first century went into effect in 1983. Today, years later, we might ask: How much of the surplus have we banked for the baby boomers? Is there a trillion or more in the kitty?

Stop dreaming. The answer is not one red cent, or even a quarter-sized Susan B. Anthony dollar.

The federal government decided to "borrow" (read "steal") the Social Security surplus on a regular basis and forget about tomorrow. In its infinite chicanery, they have been putting the FICA surplus into the General Fund and using *all of it.*

Not for the aged, or even for the aged-to-be. Instead, they've been spending the FICA surplus to pay the current bills of government, whether for White House limos or rich farmers' subsidies, or checks in the mail to 5 million unwed mothers.

How large could this federal pilfering be? Ten, 20 billion?

Guess again. It's been enormous. In 1994, the Social Security receipts alone produced a surplus of $57 billion, every dollar of which was put in the General Fund, then spent.

Since 1983, the taxmeisters *have taken—as of January 1, 1995—$413,431,000,000 (that's billions) from the Old Age and Survivors Insurance Trust Fund, or Social Security, as reported by the Bureau of the Public Debt.* (Yes, there is one.)

For those who enjoy the minutiae of legal swindles, the government even tells us where the money *appears* to be. The money is in ten sets of federal bonds: including $37 billion in 8 percent due 1996; $3 billion in 13.75 percent notes due from 1996 to 1999, and the last of which is $61 billion in 8.25 percent notes expiring in 2008. By the time the baby boomers come on line, the bonds will carry dates like 2035.

So what's the problem? The money is safe in federal bonds backed by the "full faith and credit" of the United States government, isn't it?

Of course not. As I've said, the money only *appears* to be there. Those federal bonds, or certificates of indebtedness, are nonliquid IOUs which have become part of the $4.9 trillion debt. When will that be paid back? Not before Washington, D.C., secedes from the Union, if ever.

The problem with the 1983 "save" is that it put no safeguards on the "trust fund," a nonexistent government fantasy. That was also the great failure of FDR, who never segregated Social Security money from the avaricious General Fund.

The money is all gone. To get it back, the Social Security system will have to be "saved" for the second time. Unless they stop taking the Social Security surpluses, which will average about $75 billion a year for the next decade, they'll have to raise the FICA taxes to at least 20 percent of all payrolls, with probably no maximum on the salary limit.

Or they'll have to cut the benefits and retirement age way back, perhaps to seventy. Or both. Or they'll have to borrow trillions to redeem the bonds, which will shoot interest rates way up and push the national debt into the $10 trillion range.

I MUST STRESS THAT NONE OF THIS IS THE FAULT OF THE PRESENT RECIPIENTS OF SOCIAL SECURITY BENEFITS.

Their benefits are less than the FICA payees are

"contributing." The guilt belongs to the politicians who are continuing to spend the surplus FICA money on everything but the aged, or the future aged.

What really has happened to Social Security is a funny, if tragic, scenario.

They raised the taxes to get the surplus, then spent the surplus, then they will have to raise the FICA taxes again to get a new surplus, which they'll spend again . . . ad infinitum.

Disgusted with the results of the 1983 "reform," Senator Moynihan has asked for a sizeable cut in our FICA taxes. Since we're not saving the money we might as well give it back to taxpayers, he said. His request was greeted with howls from both sides of the aisle, who know how badly they need the surplus FICA money to support their Washington mammoth.

Some would like to make the Social Security fiasco into a generational fight of oldies against youngies. But it's not. It's the American people against the American politicians. And there's still hope, as we shall see, to fix it for everyone.

The Beltway bandits have had another, rather nefarious, motive in using the FICA surplus each year. It is to make the deficit look smaller than it really is.

The 1994 deficit turned out to be $193 billion, not the $160 billion predicted by the White House. But the actual deficit is about $100 billion more. The interest on the money taken by Washington from the various "trust funds" is not counted on the deficit, as it must be.

To keep people out of jail, it has to be counted somewhere. So in the Washington world of triple-entry bookkeeping, they just add the money to the national debt, which is now approaching $5 trillion—a mathematical gimmick that makes tax cheats look sophmoric by comparison.

Ponzi is the name of the swindler who took in vast amounts of money, promising great returns with a pyramid scheme that eventually collapsed into a pile of worthless IOUs. We don't mean to compare Uncle Sam with swindlers who spent time in the can, but the present method of spending the Social Security surpluses, then borrowing more money to make good, does smell faintly reminiscent.

With all its chicanery, does the Social Security system at least deliver a decent pension?

Of course not. The maximum take home for a retiree is now about $1,400 a month, but that's not usual. As of 1995, the average retirement check is only $698, not enough to live on, unless you like dog food.

The reason, of course, is that unlike the pension plan of IBM, or the schoolteachers, or anyone else, the Social Security money has never really been invested.

The government is even scheming to get back part of that tiny pension by taxing it! In 1993, 50 percent of the Social Security benefits were taxed as income, the opening wedge in turning it into a welfare program.

By 1994, as a result of the administration's tax bill, Congress and the president increased that taxable amount of the Social Security check to 85 percent in the case of "rich" retirees with an income over $34,000, and couples with income over $44,000. That grabbed billions from the already-assaulted Social Security beneficiaries.

Is there an honest solution to the Social Security problem?

Yes, there is. It's aimed at getting Social Security out of the clutches of politicians, who cannot be trusted with our pensions. The plan is not overly complicated, costs nothing, and even Washington might be able to understand it.

The first step is to get the money as far away as possible from Congress and the president. They say Social Security is going "off budget," but that's just more Washington doubletalk. What's needed is a separate, quasi-public Social Security Retirement Board—somewhat like the Federal Reserve—which will be *totally independent* and run by a Board of Governors, including proven investment experts, appointed by the president and confirmed by Congress.

They will handle the money, invest it, set the rates of FICA taxes and retirement benefits given out. How will they operate?

1. They will not permit any more "borrowing" of the Social Security surplus by the government.

2. They will convert the Social Security system into a pure pension operation, not the hybrid of pension and welfare it is now.

3. No means tests will be involved in any way.

4. People will be allowed to earn as much as they want and still receive their benefits. (Right now a retired millionaire gets his full check, but a working man of sixty-eight who earns $35,000 a year gets nothing! Ridiculous.)

5. They will set the retirement age.

6. For the first time in history, they will truly invest Social Security funds, starting with the surplus and hoping to build a kitty for 2020.

7. The surplus money will be invested in any operation explicitly or implicitly guaranteed by the federal or state governments; Sally Mae, Freddie Mac, Ginnie Mae, and other such quasigovernmental corporations. Of course, the money will also go into *negotiable* Treasury notes and bonds, which they can buy and sell whenever they want. (Private investors now trade $1.7 *trillion* a year in Treasury securities!)

8. We should move toward "Individualization" of Social Security and true investment. (Read on.)

Had we been doing that all along, our senior citizens would now be very well off. Freddie Mac, the Federal Home Loan Mortgage Corporation, went public in 1984, and its shares have gone from $5 to a present $50, a 1,000 percent gain. Fannie Mae, the Federal National Mortgage Association, has gone from $8 in 1985 to $60 today, and has been paying good dividends all along.

How much would such an investment produce from the Social Security surplus if Uncle Sam no longer expropriated it?

If the average surplus of $75 billion a year is invested over the next twenty-five years, that's almost $2 trillion in principal. With just 6 percent interest compounded from the beginning, there will be $4.115 *trillion* in the bank by 2020—instead of nothing.

The result? Baby boomers will be getting *more* in real dollars, not less than present retirees!

Why don't we do it immediately? Because Washington has no peer in wrongheadedness when it comes to the people's money.

Are there nations that know what they're doing with their pension money? Absolutely. One sterling example is Chile. After shaking off Marxist rule, then going through a military dictatorship, they've emerged as an outstanding democratic free market nation.

What are they doing with their Social Security money? Just making 14 percent per year, that's all.

The Chilean system is becoming a model for the world. In 1981, they allowed their people to opt out of the government system and put their Social Security payments into one of fourteen authorized private pension systems. The funds were invested in stocks, bonds, bank deposits, and government-guaranteed investments. Ironically, much of it went into American securities!

The first-ten-year results are in, and they show a 14 percent annual gain. If there was only a 6 percent return, retirees would have a pension equal to 70 percent of their former salaries, a nice nest egg. But if the 14 percent gain keeps up, a lot of rich older Chileans will be clogging the streets of Disney World and walking the decks of elegant cruise ships.

The Chilean government regulates the funds, much as our SEC now regulates the stock market, and it ensures a minimum pension if a private fund fails.

Can the system work here? Of course it can. First we need to start the independent quasipublic system I spoke of and invest the surplus. Then, a little at a time, we can go the Chilean route by moving the youngest people into what is called "Privatization" of Social Security, but which I prefer to call "Individualization."

As the older retirees pass away, the plan will move in stages—perhaps over twenty years—into something very similar to the Chilean system.

Each employee will have his own account number, and his pension will be accruing to him *personally* over the years through investment, either by the Social Security Retirement Board or through investment groups as in Chile.

Whatever exact plan we follow, the present Social Security system is on a collision course with bankruptcy. We have to take a new road—and soon.

The forced savings of employees and employers over fifty years of work should produce a lot more than $698 a month.

Perhaps someday, with a lot of hard thinking, our senior citizens from the greatest nation in the world can dream of becoming as wealthy as our Chilean cousins.

Meanwhile, if politicians refuse to make the changes we desperately need, especially curbing the theft of our annual Social Security surplus, we can always pick up on Moynihan's idea and cut the FICA taxes by 20 percent and pocket the money.

Only in America.

33

TAXPAYER'S RIGHTS

Almost None

Congressman James A. Traficant, Democrat of Ohio, thought he had the IRS beat.

"Guilty until you prove yourself innocent" has been the agency byword since it began business some eighty years ago. But Traficant has for years felt that the IRS was using this apparently unconstitutional edict—a weapon given to them by the Congress itself—as a bludgeon to beat up on honest taxpayers.

A gutsy, outspoken politician, he let the IRS have it in a recent letter to colleagues, seeking their support in what just a few years ago would have been considered a quixotic gesture.

"The IRS is an agency out of control," he wrote to

his fellow House members. "All too often the IRS terror-
izes and threatens taxpayers. Too many lives have been
ruined unjustly, and it's time to rein in the IRS and insure
that it respects the rights of every taxpayer."

His anger was not a fleeting emotion. Traficant had
done his homework and introduced H.R. 390, dated January 4, 1995, which states its purpose very succinctly:

*"A bill to amend the Internal Revenue Code of 1986
to provide that the burden of proof shall be on the Secretary of the Treasury in all tax cases, and for other
purposes."*

This would totally change the behavior of the Tax
Court, the only federal court system which blatantly violates the Constitution. As Traficant's bill points out, the
IRS reverses the order of American jurisprudence to create a frightening scenario in which the taxpayer is guilty
until he can prove himself innocent.

How did his colleagues react to this invitation to tax
revolution—to make the taxpayer the innocent party in all
disputes until proven otherwise?

For years, members of both Houses have been in ab-
ject fear of the IRS, the kind of terror one associated with
J. Edgar Hoover, who held politicians at bay with his
veiled threats of blackmail. In the case of the IRS, the
leverage was more subtle, the fear of audit, hounding,
and seizure of money or property—and the resulting destruction of a political career.

*For years that fear worked well enough to keep
members of the House and the Senate quiet and docile.*

But the work of Senator David Pryor, Democrat of
Arkansas, who held hearings in 1987 and introduced the

first Taxpayer Bill of Rights, which was passed in 1988, had changed the tenor of the chambers. Revolt was plainly in the air.

How many members of the House did Traficant attract to his bill?

One hundred or more? Try 263—forty-five more than a majority! It looked like a done deal for the American people, a way out of at least some of the oppression, fiscal as well as psychological, visited on them by the IRS all these years.

But there was a hidden obstacle in its path. The bill went into the House Ways and Means Committee, which has jurisdiction over all tax matters, and was referred in turn to a subcommittee that handles the IRS, chaired by Congresswoman Nancy Johnson, Republican of Connecticut.

The hearings were held on Friday, March 24, 1995, and among the witnesses were the current IRS director and her three predecessors.

"All of them testified vehemently against the congressman's bill," recalled an aide to Traficant. "So much so that Mrs. Johnson said that she was 'impressed' by their testimony, that it would make their job of collecting taxes that much more difficult. What Congressman Traficant says is that it would have forced them to obey the Bill of Rights and they don't like that."

So what is the upshot of the Traficant attempt?

"It seems that Mrs. Johnson is going to kill our bill," the aide continued. "I don't think it will ever get out of committee."

But what is obvious is that the fight between law-abiding Americans and the IRS has been joined at the highest levels.

Back in 1987, the struggle began in the Congress when Senator Pryor, then chairman of the Senate Finance Subcommittee on Internal Revenue Service Oversight, held hearings on his proposed Taxpayer Bill of Rights.

Witness after witness—all honest American taxpayers—paraded their tales of woe, how IRS action had nearly destroyed their lives.

To any observer it became obvious that the American taxpayer had about as many rights as a Christian in the ancient Coliseum. Amendments Four and Five of the Bill of Rights, designed to protect us against search and seizure of our papers and our property without due process of law, seemed to be a foreign dicta which had no bearing in America.

In San Francisco, a retired postal worker sent his $1,300 mortgage payment to his bank, but by mistake it was delivered to the IRS office in Fresno.

Did they return the check which was made out to the bank?

No. The IRS merely altered the name of the payee and deposited it, claiming he had owed $300 in back taxes. They had never sent him a deficiency notice, and gave him no warning the check would be altered—which is illegal—or that his money would be seized.

In Las Vegas, a woman had her salary attached and a lien placed on her house because the IRS was trying to collect $92,000 owed them by her ex-husband. There was only one problem. She wasn't married to him when he ran up the debt.

In California, a ten-year-old girl had earned $694 collecting cans and doing household chores and put it in a savings account. When her father couldn't pay the $1,000 he owed the IRS—all fairly disclosed on his return—they just went in and took *her* money out of the bank.

One of those who testified was a former IRS agent, who recalled a case that gave the congressmen IRS-hives. He told of a struggling New York City model who was scheduled for an audit examination at the local IRS office. She called an IRS agent at the office to say that she was too frightened to come in personally and that she had asked someone to represent her, which is her right. The financial statement that the IRS had asked her to fill out was in the mail.

What happened? The agent, perhaps piqued to anger by her not coming in person, wiped out her bank account.

In Denver, a developer of inner-city housing voluntarily came forward to let the IRS know that his new company had made a mistake—they had failed to pay payroll taxes for three quarters. He had thought he could do it once a year, but his accountant set him straight. He had his first interview with an agent who, says the builder, told him it would be for information gathering.

When he got there, they wanted him to sign a form agreeing to a 100 percent penalty.

When he refused, the agent got angry and told him he had ten days to pay the back taxes. That was all right with the taxpayer, who was going to arrange payment. But the IRS didn't wait. Within two hours of the meeting, the IRS began seizing his bank account, which nearly pushed him into personal bankruptcy.

The stories are endless, and they have come by the hundreds and thousands into the offices of members of Congress. Some, however, seem almost unbelievable, as if they happened elsewhere and not in America.

A day-care center owed the IRS $14,000 in back taxes. A large group of IRS agents swooped down on the facility one morning and placed the children, some as young as eighteen months of age, in two rooms. Then they put tables in front of the rooms and asked the parents coming for their children to either pay the IRS then and there or sign promissory notes before picking up the youngsters!

"It was something out of a police state," says one of the mothers.

The result of Senator Pryor's hearings was the Taxpayer Bill of Rights I. It did not shift the balance of power to citizens, but it did bring in some rights to counterbalance IRS power—as if our Christian was given a switchblade to fight the lion.

What the bill does for taxpayers is:

1. If you are audited and appear in person, you can stop the examination and ask to reschedule it so that a representative—CPA, attorney, or an "enrolled agent"—can speak for you.

2. You can make an audiotape of the audit examination.

3. If the Tax Court decides in your favor, you may be able to recover some of your expenses.

4. You may be able to receive an installment agree-

ment to pay off your taxes, *but* if the IRS determines that collecting the tax is at risk, they can cancel it.

5. You can get a lien against you released if you paid the amount due before the lien was filed, or the IRS made an error, or they assessed the lien in violation of the automatic stay provisions in a bankruptcy case.

6. Your personal residence cannot be seized by ordinary action, but it can be seized with the approval of a district director or assistant director. Most important, the IRS agents—without top approval—can seize your home *if* they think collecting the tax may be at risk. That is called a "jeopardy" seizure.

7. Your bank account and property can be seized *unless you are on welfare*.

8. If your bank account is levied, the bank will hold your account for twenty-one days, which gives you time to pay the IRS bill, or set up an installment agreement.

9. If you feel you are going to suffer "hardship" you can fill out Form 911 and ask for relief on your case from a Problem Resolution Officer, or the Tax Ombudsman—who *may* or may not issue a Taxpayer Assistance Order (TAO).

10. The ombudsman is a new position established by the Taxpayer Bill of Rights. Unfortunately, this officer is named by the IRS and reports to it.

11. You will *generally* get thirty days notice before a levy or seizure unless the IRS believes the property is in jeopardy.

12. IRS agents will not be promoted based on how much money they collect, as was often the case.

There are some twenty points altogether and it has

been of some limited value to honest taxpayers. But Senator Pryor and other IRS critics now realize it is far from enough. As he says, "It was a good *first* step." But IRS abuse of power in dealing with honest taxpayers is still prevalent.

It is obvious that too much power still resides in the hands of the IRS and not enough with taxpayers. Most important, the supposed restrictions on the IRS are not mandatory in many cases, and the ombudsman—supposedly the taxpayer's last resort—is really just another employee of the IRS.

Pryor is now convinced we need a Taxpayer Bill of Rights II, or T-2, as it is informally called on the Hill.

One important aspect of the new bill is to change the taxpayer's access to someone on *his* side—maybe. Right now, the IRS Problem Resolution Officers, who try to iron out taxpayer problems, are hired, supervised, and promoted by the local district directors, who are more interested in cash coming in than protection of taxpayers.

T-2 will set up a new Office of Taxpayer Advocate, to whom the Problem Resolution Officers (PROs, who can be contacted through your local IRS office) will directly report. The Taxpayer Advocate will report to Congress twice a year on how the IRS is performing in protecting taxpayer rights, including the twenty most frequent problems faced by taxpayers and how the IRS is handling them.

Other provisions:

1. Hardships no longer have to be "significant" for a Problem Resolution Officer to take action.

2. A Taxpayer Assistance Order, which previously

could only stop IRS action, can now be used to take positive action on the taxpayer's behalf.

3. The Taxpayer Advocate can himself waive penalties.

These and other reforms may pass the Congress, but no matter what is done, they cannot change the basic problem with the IRS system. They can still waive any of the taxpayer rights passed by Congress if they—*unilaterally*—believe the collection is in jeopardy. They can then proceed to lien, levy, and seize with the speed of light without notification!

Furthermore, the entire IRS operation—set up by Congress—is still unconstitutional because it permits daily violation of Amendments Four and Five of the Bill of Rights.

How can that be stopped? By Congress, of course. But there still seem to be insufficient guts among members to proceed so dramatically, as the Traficant defeat showed.

IRS abuse could also be stopped by the courts, but they have been derelict in their duty—individually and collectively—in not protecting the people against violations of due process when it comes to liens, levies, and seizures.

The courts, including the Supreme Court, know they are winking at the Constitution when they support the IRS, as they have done time after time. Obviously they are not operating in the judicial arena in this matter, but in the political one. The Constitution is only ten pages long, and even the Justices know how to read.

But how would it look to the bureaucracy, from the

president on down, if they were just to wipe out the IRS as they did with segregation? Race is one thing, but money?

Why, then, don't citizens sue the federal government, or even the IRS, for violating their constitutional rights?

Most people don't know it, but you can't sue the United States without its permission, which is seldom granted. And permission has never been granted in a tax case. You must instead sue an individual or group, after which the Supreme Court can then issue a constitutional decision—if it wants to.

This is what happened in the segregation case of *Brown* v. *Board of Education* and in the abortion case, *Roe* v. *Wade* (Wade was then state attorney for Texas), which then became constitutional guidelines for the nation.

But the Supreme Court refuses to do the same in the case of the IRS. The furthest they have gone in the much-quoted *Bivens* v. *Six Unknown Named IRS Agents* case in 1971, was to permit citizens to sue IRS agents. But the Court has not—and apparently will not—make it a constitutional issue affecting the entire power of the IRS.

There is a case in Los Angeles now, in which a company is suing a number of agents for $1 billion for violation of constitutional rights. The attorney is confident it will result in a $100 million victory for his clients. But, he points out, "the federal government will just pay the judgment and the agents will get off scot-free."

What then is the remedy for the abusive and unconstitutional power of the IRS?

Apparently there is only one.

For Congress to close down the whole operation—shut, completely, totally—never to have it resurface in the future history of America.

34

TELEPHONE AND CABLE TAXES

Watch Out for the Info Superhighway

Everybody's getting into the act.

Cable companies will soon be competing with the local Baby Bells by providing telephone service over the same line that brings television programs into your home.

Phone companies are gearing up to provide all kinds of entertainment and shopping services through the home telephone—DIAL-A-MOVIE, ETC.

With the help of satellites, beepers, faxes, digital television, computers, cellular phones, mobile phones, personal wireless phones, wireless everything, modems, CD-ROM, it's all coming together into a CYBERSPACE NETWORK, or INFORMATION SUPERHIGHWAY, as Al Gore likes to call it.

What's this got to do with taxes and Uncle Sam?
Potentially everything.

Right now, whether you know it or not, there's a 3
percent tax on your phone bill, a federal excise tax that
was approved by the Common Carrier division of the
FCC and administered by Internal Revenue. That "small"
tax now costs us almost $2 billion a year and goes into
the federal treasury to help pay for the waste. (That's on
top of your state and local sales tax on all phone bills.)

But that may be only the beginning. Services only
now being dreamed up might soon be taxed when the
phone companies or other telecommunications operators
become the nexus of the superhighway.

*If history is any guide, the IRS and/or the FCC will
be taxing us for the use of everything from encyclopedia
research to home shopping to movies which will come
into our homes over a cable, or phone line, or modem, or
wireless connection, or all four.*

The *taxmeisters* will have something new to get their
fiscal claws into.

Many don't know it, but there's already an FCC-
sponsored tax that we're paying on our cable television
service. Washington mandated that the cable companies
had to pay a "Franchise Fee" or a "Gross Receipts Tax"
to local governments to repay them for the use of the
right-of-way (streets, etc.) to bring their wires into the 60
million homes that now have cable.

Sounds legit, but in this case, the FCC violated consumers' rights. They're permitting the cable companies to
pass the tax directly onto the cable user, as long as it's
listed separately on the bill, which it is.

Courtesy of Uncle Sam and his FCC, the cable companies collect the tax from you and use it to pay off their obligations to various local governments.

So once more we're victims of Washington mandates. Is it peanuts?

Hardly. It's $1.117 billion (that's *billion*) a year, and of course, it's not deductible from your federal or state taxes. (Case #106 of double federal taxation!) It's good for the cable companies, and bad for Mr. and Mrs. TV Viewer, and a new twist on the game of Washington extortion.

This is far from the end of the FCC's dip into your pocket. They're now taking a "fee" (read "tax") of 37 cents from the cable companies for every subscriber. In fact, they've already put in a request to raise it to 51 cents.

Who do you think will pay for it? Naturally, you, the home viewer.

There's still another hidden communications tax, this one outside the purview of the IRS, and virtually unknown to us suckers.

It's a $3.50 a month "Subscriber Line Charge" put on everyone's phone by the Federal Communications Commission. (This is in addition to the 3 percent federal excise tax.)

It started with a $1 charge for phone users in 1985 ($6 for businesses), then was raised to $3.50 for home subscribers. That's $42 a year for each telephone number, a tax that takes some $3 billion a year out of our fiscal pockets. If you have two numbers and perhaps a fax, that's $126 a year FCC tax just for the privilege of using the lines.

These three telephone and cable taxes are already up to some $6 billion a year, which is merely a head start for the IRS and the FCC as they plan for the electronic future.

As the information superhighway leaps from Al Gore's imagination into a working road with an exit in our homes, Uncle Sam will be looking carefully at a $500-billion-a-year industry.

Surely, they're sharpening their computer software to see where and how to set up an electronic toll gate for you and me.

Just a warning, fellow citizens. Watch out the next time you sit down to use your modem. The tax man may be lurking.

35

UNDERGROUND ECONOMY

The Sneaky Americans

In California, a taxpayer filed a return with such a low income figure that he claimed a $300 Earned Income Tax Credit, the welfare program that's one of the fastest-growing sources of tax fraud.

Whatever one thinks of the EITC program, at least it's supposed to be for the working poor. Was this fellow one of them?

Hardly. He had a thriving cash income on the side, large enough to buy a $17,000 hunk of shining gold bullion!

CASH. CASH. CASH.

That's the perennial cry of those who have no intention of telling the IRS how much they really take in.

In any economy you'll have your percentage of
evaders, but as tax burdens go up, the "cash people" become more active. In America today, it appears to be an
epidemic. As taxes push some people up against the fiscal wall, temptation increases to retreat into the oldest
business system of all—the Underground Economy, or, as
some call it, the "Off-the-Books" world.

It flourishes everywhere in the nation, but in the
good old days of insignificant taxes (World War II and
Korean War vets remember), it was small and easily ignored. But not today.

The plumber, the street vendor, the home improvement contractor, the owner of sweatshops, carpenters,
even doctors and lawyers—anyone who will accept cash,
or checks made out to "Cash"—make up what is believed
to be a thriving $500- to $750-billion-a-year industry,
taking as much as 10 percent of the Gross Domestic
Product.

Some call it an "informal" economy because it provides work for people who would not otherwise be employed, or solvent, if they paid taxes, or taxes were paid
on their behalf.

*It's also the fastest-growing segment of our economy,
rising some 8 percent a year while legitimate business is
lucky to go up 3 percent.*

This, of course, does not include the true criminal
world, which would add another $200 billion or so. It's
safe to predict that given today's tax structure, the Underground Economy will continue to grow rapidly—unless
the whole tax structure is dramatically reformed.

It doesn't take a CPA to understand that such a thriving subterranean world could eventually threaten the aboveboard operation.

How much does Uncle Sam lose from the hidden economy?

Estimates vary, but a conservative number—what the IRS calls the "tax gap"—is some $127 billion a year. Others believe that's only part of the story.

It's also a cumulative spiral. As more people believe that others are cheating, there's a tendency to do the same by entering the cash economy. And the complexity of the tax code doesn't help either. People either feel inadequate to understand and deal with it, or feel unable to pay for it.

Some of them give up completely, yielding to the easy temptations of the Underground world. In Texas, the deputy comptroller estimated that $50 billion of the state's economy was "off books."

The gap between rich and poor, which has been accelerating, leads to more hidden cash. Poor self-employed people work for the richer ones, who now want more and more services. The workers, in turn, ask for cash to keep their taxes down and make up for their reduced position in life. This tendency is fed by increased immigration, which brings more people into the service sector, the heart and soul of the Underground Economy.

New York City authorities have estimated that it's costing the city $1 billion a year in lost taxes, and they're trying to crack down.

Their first goal was nonfilers, people who just didn't send in the city's income tax form. Computer matching of returns against lists such as licenses, unincorporated business tax filers, even lists from the IRS, turned up 18,000 nonfilers, and an additional $34 million in taxes.

Immigrants, with cash-only or part-cash jobs, play a large part in the Underground Economy. Samuel Ehrenhalt, regional commissioner of the Bureau of Labor Statistics, believes earnings statistics of immigrant income are 10 to 20 percent smaller than reality.

Immigrant neighborhoods have large pools of willing workers and ingenious entrepreneurs, which also increases the untaxed cash flow. The mixture spells "Underground." Often contractors pick up these immigrants, many of whom are illegal, in the morning, then transport them to affluent suburban towns where they work for $4 or $5 an hour "off the books."

The International Ladies Garment Workers Union, which has lamented the decline of the legitimate apparel business in New York, indicates that the Underground clothing business, fueled by immigrants, is thriving. They believe there are 3,000 untaxed apparel factories (including classic "sweatshops") in the New York area as against only 200 in 1970.

Which businesses nationwide tend to go Underground to avoid taxes?

Researchers at the IRS think it's centered in certain industries, including some unexpected ones:

1. Passenger transportation, such as limos and taxicabs
2. Roofing construction
3. Used car dealers
4. Producers
5. Orchestras and entertainers

6. Direct selling organizations
7. Miscellaneous personal services

Other areas where cash is king include car repairs, child care, street vending, part-time bookkeeping, sales, and restaurant work, especially tips.

Of course, Underground people, who save on taxes, lose their Social Security and Unemployment Insurance benefits, but that doesn't seem to slow them down.

Cash is king in some higher-income businesses as well. The IRS found that one prominent ballplayer was pocketing the cash from convention appearances. One family was found to be dealing in unreported cash from admission charges at their folk art shows.

The IRS believes a lot of the Underground activity comes from among the self-employed, claiming that 500,000 of them making over $25,000 a year don't even file returns, evading $7 billion in federal taxes, plus at least as much in Social Security and state taxes.

Is there any way to catch the cash-lovers?

High-speed computer workstations are being called into play by the IRS. The gold-bug who was on tax welfare was caught by the Currency and Banking Retrieval System, a method of tracking cash transactions of $10,000 or more.

One computer work-through found that one in five of the people who had used cash to buy big-ticket items such as cars and planes hadn't even filed a 1040!

The computer bases available for double-checking are numerous: property transfers, for instance. A check of

New York records found that 18 percent of those required to file gift tax returns "forgot" to do so.

Will the Underground Economy ever be eliminated by the IRS and its sister collectors in the states?

Not as long as we have a system based on income taxes.

Pressures for a larger Underground Economy will continue to rise as long as the cost of life goes up more than stated inflation; household income remains static; taxes like Social Security rise yearly; and immigration continues to grow.

Fiscal oppression just naturally leads to tax evasion.

So what to do?

Simple. Nobody can evade what's not there.

The only answer, as we shall see, is that in a free society, it's nobody's business how much money you make.

No one should have to confess their income to any government or be unconstitutionally forced to keep receipts, or produce papers, or give up their property in default of taxes.

That, of course, requires the legal abolition of the IRS and all state and city income taxes as well, a goal for the next four years.

Without it, the Underground Economy will not only remain with us, but will get progressively larger.

It's your country. Only you can fix it.

36

VALUE ADDED TAX (VAT)

The Wrong Way to Go

VAT FOR THE USA?

I hope not.

Virtually every nation in Europe has a VAT tax, which is basically a hidden or "invisible" tax. That's the reason politicians like it. It brings in an enormous amount of revenue silently, without raising the ire of people who can't see it in action. Eventually, of course, it weakens the economy and does it damage—this time more "visibly."

How does it work?

The VAT is a tax at every stage of production, whether a car or a submarine sandwich at your local deli. A vast army of new IRS (or VAT) agents would check businesses as they progress in creating a product, then tax them as they go. The businesses would in turn add the several taxes they paid to the government to the final price of the product—apparently without the consumer noticing it.

(Americans who travel abroad are familiar with the VAT, because as foreigners they are exempt from the tax. Once they're back in the states, they receive a refund if they've applied for it overseas.)

So what's wrong? More money coming in to Uncle Sam "invisibly" and "painlessly"?

Don't hold your breath. President Clinton, for one, looked enviously at the VAT taxes used in Europe, and made tentative plans to hook America into the system to pay for the now-aborted national health scheme. Talk is that White House insiders were considering a giant VAT on goods, beginning in 1995–96 to pay for the scheme.

Advocates of the VAT say that it would be perfect, making it possible to cut down other taxes. Also, the new money coming in would quickly balance the budget. A 5 percent VAT, for example, would bring in some $220 billion in five years.

The reality, of course, is that a VAT tax appeals to theorists because it brings in enough money for them to enormously expand the government and make it more palatable to the unknowing.

In fact, the White House is salivating over the prospect right now. President Clinton has hinted at the possibility of a federal VAT tax in an interview with *Fortune*. Both Leon Panetta, chief of staff at the White House, and Alice Rivlin, head of the Office of Management and Budget, have made complimentary noises about their dream of gaining new revenue so easily. Apparently, only the change in control of the Congress has held them back.

Caveat emptor. Buyer beware.

So what's the trouble with VATs? It sounds good, but there are several fateful loopholes which change the "invisible" tax into a potential nightmare.

One is that when VAT has been used in Europe, it has mainly been *added* to taxes instead of replacing them. It also raises taxes, silently, but dangerously.

The problem is that VAT's very invisibility tends to make its rates go higher and higher. Austria brought in an 8 percent VAT in 1973. Today it's 20 percent. Denmark began its VAT at 10 percent in 1967, and now it's 22 percent. Britain went from 10 percent to its present 17.5; Italy from 12 to 19. You get the idea.

A study of VAT countries showed that their average national tax burden was 44 percent of their GDP versus only 32 percent in non-VAT nations.

Another problem is the rise in the price of goods and the inflation and unemployment that follows. The Congressional Budget Office estimates that a 5 percent VAT tax would result in a 3 percent jump in inflation, with the bad news and higher interest rates that brings. Those interest rates can turn a prosperity into an unwelcome recession.

What is the answer?

We need one less, not one more, tax system. Scrap the VAT idea. Otherwise, like Europe, we'll end up with both!

Majority Leader Dick Armey, the prime advocate of

a flat tax, is against the VAT concept, and is leading a 125-member caucus against it in the House.

We can't be diverted in the crusade to save America. As we shall see, there's only one direction for a better tomorrow: the end of the IRS.

37

WITHHOLDING TAX

They Like It in Their Bank

It was a stroke of genius for World War II. Mr. Ruml, whose name has now gone into infamy, devised the plan to withhold federal taxes from almost everyone's paycheck—an "emergency" measure begun in 1942 solely to pay for the war.

That war is over, as is the Korean, the Vietnam, the Gulf, and even the aborted Haitian escapade, but the system is still there and entrenched, like it or not.

Of the $543 billion raised in individual federal income taxes in 1994, some 70 percent was withheld at the source, right on the job site.

It's called "painless" tax paying, but it can better be described as the use of general anesthesia to do radical surgery—on your paycheck. Sweat money is being taken from us, but since it's deducted in advance it's as if we never got it. Or so the federal propaganda goes.

(People still talk about making $60,000 a year, when they're lucky to be taking home $40,000.)

A tax is a tax whenever they take it. In fact, rather paradoxically, "painless" withholding is probably at the core of our whole government mess. If Washington had to collect the money after the fact, as localities do, the cash wouldn't be there to pay for the government's irrational excesses. Without that ready withholding cash—which never existed before World War II—the brakes would have been put on the federal boondoggle long ago.

States watch Washington, then imitate the federal big boys. They've also put in withholding, which collects some $200 billion a year in forty-three states—still more "painless" surgery on your paycheck. (If it gets any more painless, the patient will become numb.)

Many people are anesthetized against the withholding hit because of tax refunds—when the IRS returns money they should never have taken in the first place. Eighty-one million individuals receive refunds totaling $83 billion, or a little over $1,000 each.

It seems to be a time of joy for these innocent taxpayers. Actually, they should be outraged at one of the great ripoffs of all time. The IRS has borrowed the money from the taxpayer, deposited it, and earned the interest themselves. But when it comes to refunding the money, they pay the taxpayer *no interest*. The IRS really has taken an interest-free loan through the overpayment of withholding, and they've gotten away with it.

(Of course, if a taxpayer is short on his payment, he's charged 8 percent interest on the shortfall, plus penalties.)

Since the government has held the $83 billion for an average of six months, at 8 percent interest they should be paying taxpayers an additional $3.2 billion each year in interest for the use of the money.

It's a nice scheme, but then no one has ever accused the IRS of fairness.

(The only time the IRS pays interest on refunds is when they are more than forty-five days late in sending them out. The interest is then only for that short extended period.)

The withholding amount is figured from the W-4 form, the Employee's Withholding Allowance Certificate. The employee checks off the number of dependents (each worth $2,450), but he can check more if there are large offsetting deductions—like large mortgage interest, state or local taxes, or deductible business losses.

But if he checks more than ten, the IRS is supposed to be notified, with an explanation. If the IRS thinks you're *deliberately* taking too many deductions, they can fine you $500.

Of course, there's also a penalty for shortfall if the total withheld is less than 90 percent of your actual tax bill at the end of the year. (That penalty will not be enforced if your withholding equals the full tax you paid the year before.)

One taxpayer, a pilot who had a $40,000 deduction for a business loss, listed twenty exemptions on his W-4. Unfortunately, he ignored an IRS letter asking for the reason. Quickly, they contacted his employer, who cut his deductions down to "zero." That resulted in an additional $1,800 a month withheld from his paycheck—money he needed to make up for his business loss.

Finally, after the intervention of a tax troubleshooter, his account was refigured and he was allowed thirty-four deductions for the year!

Not only salary, but sick pay and taxable fringe benefits are withheld as well. The employer can also withhold taxes on commissions, bonuses, and overtime, at the rate of 28 percent, which was upped from 20 percent as part of the president's 1993 tax hike. That's also true of certain gambling winnings, recorded on a W-2G form.

Another withholding problem is the IRS rule to hold back 20 percent on distributions of company pension plans and annuities, all marked on a W-4P. In fact, *Money* magazine has called it "a lousy law" that was invented to gain a quick $2 billion for the IRS. The withholding can be avoided by shifting a pension to still another retirement system, but it takes adroitness, including what's called a "trustee-to-trustee" transfer.

But some people need the money when they're fired or get sick. Now they're 20 percent short.

Interest and dividends can be a withholding trap as well—if you're not careful. If the disburser doesn't have your Social Security number, they're told to hold a "backup" of 31 percent. By signing Form W-9, the taxpayer can eliminate that problem.

The government is always trying to get more taxpayers on withholding. The collection is sure and they have cash to play with. One way out of withholding is to become an "independent contractor" instead of an employee.

"IC," as it is known, is a fast-growing business. Employers are relieved of dozens of regulations and withholding payments, including unemployment insurance, FICA, and income tax. The independent contractor—whether limo driver or real estate salesman—also likes it because even though he has to pay almost double Social Security taxes, he's able to deduct more expenses, including a home office.

But the IRS is fighting employers to keep them from expanding the IC ranks. It's a continuous crackdown which some employers consider IRS "harassment."

Unfortunately, withholding is probably the only present way to extract the enormous amounts Washington wants to run its bloated operation. For most salaried taxpayers, it's probably necessary as well. Otherwise, they would be paying penalties and interest to the IRS instead of paying their rent.

What's the answer?

The shame of it is that a well-run government needs considerably less money than we're now spending (see "How to Balance the Budget"). And our present extraction method—the income tax—is the wrong way to raise what's truly needed.

So the next time you curse your paycheck because of the big hole made by the IRS (and your state and local income tax), think of the day when they'll all be a memory.

Then there will be no reason to withhold anything, especially your smile.

38

X-TRA! X-TRA!

---

66 Ways to Excise You to Death!

What do the following have in common?

Fishing rods
Telephones
Inland waterways
Gasoline
Airline tickets
People who put too much money into their IRA
Chemicals
Gambling

Give up?
The answer is "absolutely nothing."

But that hasn't stopped the IRS from taxing them all under a catch-all called "excise taxes."

What does "excise" mean? The *Random House Dictionary* says it is "an internal tax or duty on certain commodities. . . . on the manufacture, sale or consumption within the country."

But the word has a second meaning as a verb: "To remove by or as if by cutting." Here we come closer to the truth—to slice away at our pocketbooks in sixty-six different ways.

The only connection among the items is that the idea was innocently ordained by the Founding Fathers. Since they prohibited income taxes in the Constitution, money had to be raised somehow. So they instituted excise taxes—as on whiskey, which led to a rebellion in Pennsylvania.

It had meaning at one time. Then the income tax became law and eventually our main source of revenue. But in the transition, no one remembered—or wanted—to shut down the excise taxes. So now we have both.

Excise taxes are chosen with no theory in mind except Washington's constant desperate need for cash to run its inefficient operation. The taxes were arrived at by historical accident and need a good shaking up today.

There are sixty-six different excise taxes, which bring in $34 billion a year by following one time-tested theory:

1. If it moves, tax it.
2. If it doesn't move, tax it.
3. If it falls in neither category, tax it.

Excise taxes follow that rule scrupulously. They work by casting out an enormous tax net that ranges from pistols to vaccines, and even to those people who put too much money in their IRAs, a tax trap which brought in $5,992,000!

The list makes extraordinary reading. The IRS handles most of it, but the firearms have been transferred to the Bureau of Alcohol, Tobacco and Firearms, an ominous-sounding operation in the Department of Treasury.

The rates on excise taxes are as haphazard as their rationale. We pay an 11 percent tax on "bows and arrows," but only 10 percent on "pistols and revolvers," and a mere 3 percent on sonar devices. All this in *addition* to state and local sales taxes.

If you visit a gun or a sporting goods shop, you won't see these taxes on the sales slip, which on an elegant $300 bow and arrow would be $33.

How come?

Because most excise taxes are hidden. They're paid to the IRS directly by the manufacturer, then buried in the price and passed on to the consumer.

A retailer of both fishing and hunting equipment was shocked to learn that excise taxes on his goods even existed. But he smiled at the government's savvy. "If we had to collect that much money from the customers, they'd scream and it would hurt my business. By taxing the manufacturer, the people don't know about it. Just as I didn't."

There's a lot we Americans don't know about our taxes. We've already seen that the airline ticket tax is a semi-hidden operation. But there are several open excise taxes—four of which we've treated separately: gasoline, sin, telephone, and luxury taxes.

The excise tax list shows the tax writers' creativity. There's a tax on foreign insurance policies, one on chemicals from as little as 22 cents a ton to $10.13 a ton. There's a 3 percent excise tax on outboard motors, then one on sonar devices, both strangely listed on the same line. There's a cruise ship passenger tax of $3 per person if they berth overnight, and a 6.25 percent tax on cargo shipped by air.

Then there's LUST. Not in the heart of Jimmy Carter but for the Leaking Underground Storage Tank fund, an excise tax on leaking gasoline.

There's also an expensive excise tax which brings in $111 million a year. That's the gas guzzler (GG) tax meant to discourage the manufacture and purchase of cars that get too few miles on a gallon and theoretically add to the air pollution. (Using supposed good motivations to extract more money from the public is an old Washington gimmick.) But the manufacturers—who make the guzzlers—don't pay for it. The consumers do.

I did a little checking and found it's expensive. The tax runs from $1,000 up to $7,700, which is quite an environmental hit.

Most of the tax applies to large, powerful, and/or expensive cars. One Mercedes dealer explained that of his major models, the SL5000 has a $1,300 gas guzzler tax, while the S600 will cost the customer $3,000 extra. (There's an even larger "luxury tax" on these expensive cars.)

The GG tax on a BMW 540 (cost $50,000) will set

you back $1,300; $1,000 on a 740, which costs $60,000
but is apparently better on gas mileage, while a BMW
840 carries a tax of $1,300. The Porsche 911 (about
$70,000) carries a $1,000 gas guzzler fee, while the 928
($82,000) runs $3,000 extra. One champion, which turns
up its hood at both the IRS and the EPA, is the Ferrari—
cost $207,000—with a GG tax of $5,400!

What about big American cars like the Lincoln or
Cadillac Brougham?

"No," say their dealers. There's no GG tax on them.
Their gas mileage is excellent, a virtue shared by Lexus,
one foreign carmaker who's proud of not being a GG.

How does the government get away with all the excise taxes that bedevil us—and whose list continues to
grow?

Simple. Over the years, the American public was
brainwashed to believe that Congress knows what it's
doing, a whimsical thought which is far off the mark.

The reality is that tax writers, including those who
inhabited the House Ways and Means Committee for
forty years, scan the horizon and pick out any number of
human activities to tax—if they can get away with it politically. If it's too hot, they merely bury the excise tax in
the manufacturer's factory instead of in the face of the
consumer.

It's a clever way around opposition, a technique Eu-
ropeans use in their VAT tax and which we're falling into.

**But what can the average citizen do about it—
hidden taxes and all?**

Read on, dear citizen and join the tax revolution.

And yes, there's really an excise tax on vaccines.

39

YACHTS AND LUXURY TAXES

Soak-It-to-the-Rich?

In 1990, during the Bush administration—when the president reneged on his "read-my-lips" promise—the government put in a giant tax increase, one that is held greatly responsible for the recession of 1991–92.

What to tax? The men with the green eyeshades in the basement of the Treasury Building pondered and came up with one idea they thought was sage.

"Soak the rich" was the byword. Luxury items were a logical target, and a 10 percent tariff was put on everything that glittered for those with loose cash.

There were five categories that, beginning in January 1, 1991, would become more expensive for those who loved, and could afford, the finer things in life:

1. Airplanes that cost over $250,000
2. Boats priced over $100,000
3. Cars/trucks/vans over $30,000
4. Jewelry over $10,000
5. Furs over $10,000

It looked like the easiest way to pick up about $400 million a year and to help reduce the burgeoning deficit. Anyway, who cared about the rich? There were fewer of them than us, and besides, they contributed nothing to the culture but charity balls and fancy divorces. And of course, a lot of taxes. (The top 1 percent pay 27 percent of all individual income taxes.)

What happened? The government put in the luxury taxes and the businesses involved died a rapid, convulsive death. It was a quick lesson for Washington and for all of us. Taxes, on anybody or anything, always kill any goose contemplating laying a golden egg. Jobs and Gross Domestic Product (GDP) *always* work the opposite of the tax rate, as the low-tax Pacific Rim countries show us every day.

The hardest hit by the luxury levy were not the rich (who just put their money into more tax-free municipals), but the people who made the goods for them, and the jobs those businesses generated.

When the tax went into effect in January 1991, the first to get hit was the boat-making business, which went into instant paralysis.

The $100,000 luxury tax exemption on new boats— which sounded like a lot to bureaucrats, was peanuts for yachts for which a million dollars is a modest price. The rich took out their calculators and learned that the federal tax was going to cost them $90,000 on a $1 million boat they docked in a U.S. harbor. Even if they bought it overseas and brought it back to Miami, they were still liable.

(Some smarties bought their boats in the United States but took delivery in the Bahamas. As long as they kept the boat "offshore," they escaped the tax. But naturally, they had less use of it.)

The effects of the boat luxury tax are still reverberating even though the tax was in existence only for 1991 and 1992. In 1993, after enormous protest, it was lifted on everything except cars.

"The tax devastated the boat industry, and we've never recovered," says Greg Proteau, spokesman for the National Marine Manufacturers Association. "The price of used boats immediately went up 10 percent. People were being laid off by boat builders by the thousands. The government started the tax to soak the rich, but they ended up soaking the workers, most of whom had made good money. We started with 50,000 employees in the boat-building industry and went down to 25,000. Now we've come back to 35,000, but I doubt that the American boat business will ever return to what it was."

His anger at our ridiculous tax policy is backed up by the numbers. Before the tax, in 1988, the industry built 12,000 boats a year selling for over $100,000—the threshold price for the IRS luxury tax.

And now? "We went down to as low as 3,400 boats, and in 1994 we only went back to 4,200. We're still way behind and I don't think we'll ever fully return."

Why did the rich so rapidly boycott products that were taxed?

"It wasn't just the money. If they bought a million-dollar boat, they could afford the tax," says Proteau. "No, it was a matter of psychology. They were angry that they were being singled out again. Instead, they put their money elsewhere—a vacation home, or a used boat, and something else, but not a high-taxed new boat."

Not only was the luxury tax on boats a disaster for American workers, but it failed the Treasury. It brought in only $16 million—a fraction of the losses suffered by the $12 billion boat business!

The aircraft industry was another victim of this idiotic tax. A study done by the General Aviation Manufacturers Association showed that seventy-four planes designed for pleasure and costing over $250,000 *would not be sold* in the three years following the beginning of the LET (Luxury Excise Tax). The loss of business in turboprop, turbojet, and helicopters was at least $60 million.

Surely that was made up for by the IRS take?

No way. All the IRS took in in 1991 was $151,000 (that's thousand), and $702,000 in 1992. During the two years it was in effect, *the plane tax brought in under $1 million, less than it cost to collect the money.*

"The aircraft manufacturers most affected by the tax were companies like Beech, Mooney, and Piper, and others," says a trade association spokesman. "Most of their planes didn't qualify for the exemption, which requires that the plane be used at least 80 percent for business."

The bauble business, which had only a $10,000 exemption, was hit as well.

"The luxury tax killed our business," says an angry Henri Barguirdjian, president of Van Cleef & Arpels. "On the high end of our sales—items selling for $50,000 or more—we dropped 60 percent in volume. I would estimate that our losses were some $30 million."

Why, I asked, would rich people care about a measly 10 percent tax?

"It was mainly psychological. If a $100,000 piece of jewelry went up from $100,000 to $110,000 because of the cost of the gems or manufacture, my customers wouldn't care. But when they had to pay an extra 10 percent luxury tax on top of an 8 percent sales tax, they just decided they wouldn't buy. Had the government been smart it would have put a small 1 percent luxury tax across the board without a $10,000 exemption. They would have collected more money and customers wouldn't have cared."

(His request for the federal government to become "smart" instead of "clever" is an exercise in fantasy.)

In August 1993, most of the luxury tax was repealed, retroactive to January 1, 1993, but not the luxury tax on cars.

Why? Because Washington saw that the luxury tax on new cars (used cars are exempt) had brought in $390 million in fiscal 1993, over 90 percent of the total!

Today, everyone from Cadillac buyers to those who buy (or lease) a Ferrari, BMW, or Mercedes pay a 10 percent luxury tax on all cars costing over $32,000. (There's also that gas guzzler excise tax on some large cars.)

Foreign cars are mainly affected, even though the buyers are American. A Porsche 928, which can cost

$82,000, carries an extra luxury tax of $5,000, as does the
S500, an $82,000 Mercedes sedan. A top-of-the-line Mer-
cedes, the S600 V-12, goes for $134,000—and carries a
luxury tax of over $10,000.

Most American cars escape the levy, but rising
prices are putting some in jeopardy. A typical Cadillac,
says a dealer, goes for $36,000. With the $32,000 exemption, the tax comes to only $400. But a Cadillac SST
is up over $50,000, with almost a $2,000 extra luxury
tax—on top of a typical $3,000 sales tax. But if we con-
sider Ford-owned Jaguar as an American car, we're talking big dollars. The XJ12 goes for $72,000, carrying a
luxury tax of $4,000.

"One of the bad features of the present luxury tax,"
says a Connecticut Mercedes dealer, "is that the federal
government doesn't count trade-ins. If someone trades in
a $52,000 Porsche toward an $82,000 Mercedes, the state
sales tax is only on the $30,000 difference. But the fed-
eral luxury tax is on the full $82,000. It makes no sense."

Sense or not, Uncle Sam always needs money.

I have two pieces of advice for our Congress:

Stop hurting the car business the way you crippled
the boat business. In a recession, they'll reel.

Failing that, the consumer should shop around for a
good, top-of-the-line used car and tell Uncle Sam to peddle his taxes you know where.

40

ZANY TAX STORIES

Believe It or Not

The whole structure of our tax system and the IRS lends itself to ridicule.

Between the enormous, undecipherable tax code, the Tax Court, the interpretations and decisions about the code by other courts—including the Supreme Court—there is little to respect, even more to laugh at.

It's not surprising that we could catalogue some zany tax stories that titillate, even infuriate, by showing how our present tax system violates everything we love about America.

We've already seen several cases of absurdities. Here are a few more for your bemusement.

1. Anglo-American tradition rejects the idea of ex

post facto laws, which bind people to laws passed after the fact.

But that's just what the president, the Congress, and the IRS did by passing the 1993 tax bill, which turned its back on accepted common law. Not only did the bill raise the tax rate to 39.6 percent (actually 42), but it made the tax hike *retroactive* to the January before.

People now owed Uncle Sam billions of dollars for money earned before the law was passed. It was an efficient scheme to both raise a lot of cash and destroy American tradition.

But, of course, pundits said, the Supreme Court—in its infinite wisdom—would never support retroactive taxation. Yet the highly overrated institution did just that. It went along with the IRS, as it usually does.

In the privacy of their minds, the jurists probably agree that the law violates everything we stand for. But like bureaucrats everywhere, they proclaim: WASHINGTON NEEDS THE MONEY!

Justice Antonin Scalia, speaking for the high court, said that their ruling in favor of President Clinton's tax scam, "guarantees that *all* retroactive tax laws will henceforth be valid."

Is there no tax justice, or is that an oxymoron?

2. What if you've paid taxes to a town or a state, and the tax is then ruled unconstitutional?

You can get your money back. Right?

Wrong. On February 22, 1994, the Supreme Court ruled that you're stuck, Constitution or no. Georgia had placed a tax on military retirees that a lower federal court ruled unconstitutional.

The taxpayers sued for return of their money and the case went all the way up to the Supreme Court.

Open and shut. Right?

No. The Supreme (God help us) Court ruled that yes, the tax was unconstitutional, but the money still didn't have to be returned to the taxpayers. They found for the hungry Georgia treasury.

Why? Because since a "predeprivation" hearing was held, the military retirees should have suspected that they were paying an unconstitutional tax. Having paid it, they had no recourse.

One wonders. Did the august men and women in black originally train as tax collection agents?

3. Native American Indians on reservations are exempt from paying taxes on cigarettes because other Indians are doing the smoking. Fine, said the tax men in New York State. But if they sell them to palefaces, they've got to charge and collect the taxes.

How would they know one customer from another? New York law now requires that Indian cigarette retailers get *written* proof from their customers that they are truly the biological descendants of the people who used to own America!

4. The Congress and its handmaiden, the IRS, are cracking down on travel expenses.

But too much is too much.

A husband and wife who drove a tractor-trailer for a

living listed their traveling expenses as a business deduction, which is quite logical. The IRS code dictates that you can collect same if you're traveling away from home on business.

The couple, who were often on the road, listed the traveling costs on Schedule C (for business) on their Form 1040, but the IRS rejected their deduction.

Why?

Because, said the IRS, they were away so much that the cab of their tractor-trailer had to be considered their real home!

5. Have you many enemies? That's bad for you and good for the IRS, which encourages stool pigeons with the lure of gold—federal tax dollars they pay out to anyone who tattletales on you.

Called IRS "informers," they could be a neighbor, a disgruntled employee, or an ex-spouse. In a recent year, the IRS paid out $5.3 million to stoolies, an average reward of $6,340 for snitching.

For information used that's responsible for recovery of tax, the informer gets 10 percent of the first $75,000, 5 percent of the next $25,000 and 1 percent of the balance. The top reward is $100,000.

Are there "regulars" in the business? Oh, yes. The IRS often deals with 800 informants, 40 of whom are accountants.

The IRS is appreciative of the work of citizens who snitch on others, just as was the KGB. But don't think that even the informers get off easy. They have to pay income taxes on the reward!

6. The Senate Finance Committee is one of the two main writers of the crazy tax code. Do they look out for themselves?

You bet your life. If your employer provides parking space and it's worth more than $155, you—the recipient—pay a tax on the difference, something that's quite possible in New York, Washington, and other big cities.

Senators park in underground parking spots on the Hill that normally cost $290 a month, which means they'd have to pay tax on the $135-a-month difference. But they were determined not to feed the IRS on taxes designed for outsiders.

What did they do? They changed the reserved $290 fee to first-come, first-served and priced it at less than $155. Thus no tax. Ingenious, what?

Talk in Washington is that other federal agencies, including the Treasury Department and its child, the IRS, are keeping the price for freebie parking at $145 a month so they can escape the new taxes as well.

Isn't it nice to write the tax laws instead of just obeying them?

7. Business interest is deductible on your income tax, but personal interest is not. If a person makes his money in a one-man business, can he deduct any interest he has to pay to the IRS for any one of a dozen reasons?

One would think so. But because we're dealing in billions, the 1986 tax law asserted—arbitrarily—that any such interest paid to the IRS was "personal." It was nondeductible even if the money earned came from a business. (Perhaps the IRS should take courses in philosophy.)

Was the IRS right? The Tax Court ruled yes, which seemed to close the case.

Suddenly, there's new news on that front. A farming family deducted their IRS interest on their Schedule F (business of farming return), which was quickly disallowed by the IRS. They went to federal district court, which decided that the 1986 "temporary" ruling was invalid. They noted that Congress used the word "generally"—and not "always"—in referring to interest paid to the IRS that could not be deducted. The federal court ruled in favor of the farm family and allowed the deduction.

So, can anyone who paid interest to the IRS get part of their money back?

Maybe. You can file Form 8275, which states that you disagree with an IRS temporary ruling. You also have to file amended returns for the years involved, asking for the deduction and a refund of the interest already paid.

Good idea? Maybe, maybe not. One tax adviser warns: When you get aggressive with the IRS, they get aggressive back, and you can expect an audit.

But I thought audits were only used to check the accuracy of returns. Foolish boy.

8. A housewife in a northern Chicago suburb answered the insistent knock on her door.

She opened it only to find *three* IRS agents demanding to see her daughter. They wanted to know why

$1,400 in savings account interest reported by a bank had not been declared by her daughter on her Form 1040. The terrified woman called her husband, who called their accountant, who called the agents to explain.

The money was a gift from the daughter's grandparents, he told the agents.

But why wasn't the woman's daughter available to personally explain that to them, the IRS agents asked?

Sorry, said the accountant. She was away for the day—in her second-grade class at school.

Three IRS agents showing up in person to check on a little girl's bank interest?

Only in America.

HOW TO FIRST BALANCE THE BUDGET, THEN . . .

The two goals of better government are inextricably linked: a smaller, more responsive operation and lower taxes.

The elimination of the IRS, which is absolutely necessary, will not by itself change the nation's fiscal dilemma. *In the beginning* we will have to raise approximately the same amount of money.

The dramatic change tax reform will bring is to free citizens from confession, filing, and dealing with an oppressive enforcement agency. It will also free up capital so that the people—not the government—can spend their money as they see fit. This will turn decision-making back to the citizens and greatly expand the economy.

But while we're changing the tax system, we must simultaneously take the next step—reversing the thirty years of bad and bloated government. This is best accomplished by dramatically downsizing Washington, which will first lead to a balanced budget, then to much lower taxes for everyone.

This chapter deals with cost cutting at the federal level. State and local governments will automatically benefit as Washington mandates less and asks for fewer cost-sharing dollars, whether for welfare or any failed federal program.

Budget cutting at the federal level will also be a perfect guide for states and localities to follow, as they must and eventually will.

My reduction plan is quite simple and attainable. I call it the "Twenty-Five Percent Solution" because it envisions a one-fourth cut in all government in America. If we take the $2.6 trillion cost of all government today—federal, state, and local—I envision that by the year 2002 we will be spending one-fourth less, or a total of only $2 trillion in today's dollars.

Instead of spending 40 percent of the Gross Domestic Product on government, we will be cutting it back to 30 percent, a sensible figure that is about the size it was some thirty years ago.

What are the benefits? First, a balanced budget, and second a 30 percent cut in taxes across the board.

Let's look at the year 2002, the year in which the Congress hopes to balance the budget, and see how much better we can do under my plan.

How do you possibly cut 25 percent out of an entrenched government like Washington?

It's quite easy. The first step is to keep Social Security out of the argument (and out of the hands of politicians) by taking it totally out of the budget and setting it up as an independent quasipublic organization in which the money, for the first time, is truly invested (see "Social Security Taxes").

This will also stop the pilfering of FICA funds to help run the rest of the government and to make the deficit appear smaller than it really is.

(An estimated $75 billion will be stolen each year until the 2002 target date unless we adopt the new independent plan.)

Going out to the year 2002, the Clinton budget envisions a growth of some 4.5 percent annually, ending with a continuous deficit of $200 billion a year.

The Republican plan envisions a growth of about 2.5 percent a year, which is expected to create a balanced budget by 2002.

Naturally, the Republican plan is much better than the president's. But from my vantage point, it is still insufficient. At the year 2002, the federal budget may well be balanced, but at too high a spending level!

My plan is more dramatic and attainable. It envisions a ZERO GROWTH for the next seven years, inflation included. *That means an actual reduction of 3.5 percent per year, or 25 percent by the target date of 2002. This will result in a $200 billion a year surplus!*

How do we accomplish that?

In my two prior books on government, *THE GOV-*

ERNMENT RACKET: Washington Waste From A to Z and *A CALL FOR REVOLUTION: How Washington Is Strangling America*, I laid out spending reform in great detail. Some of it is now in the works in the Congress, but much of it has yet to be addressed.

Since this is a book on taxation, I will only summarize the salient points of my plan and show how ZERO GROWTH will provide not only the balanced budget, but an enormous cut in taxes.

It's important to understand that the federal budget is presented to the public and the media in the form of a charade—one practiced by both Republican and Democratic presidents. Nowhere does it mention the cost of running the operation, in either salaries, pensions, or overhead, a figure, as we shall see, that equals $400 billion billion a year! Search as you will, you'll find none of that in the budget.

Instead, the budget is now organized mainly by functions in a fake pie chart, which hides many of the areas easily cut.

For example, when it speaks of entitlements, it does not mention that there are sixteen of them, most of which have nothing to do with the popular concepts of Medicare, Social Security, and Medicaid. The "entitlements" actually include all farm subsidies, defaulted loans such as the Export-Import Bank or Farmers Home Administration mortgage failures, and even corporate pension belly-ups insured by the government.

I have organized the spending cuts into eleven points, each covering a broad range of federal activities. This is only a partial list. There are hundreds of federal programs that need to be closed, but this list will provide a broad framework of cuts.

It is my firm belief that my spending reduction program and the elimination of the IRS will be the two "magic bullets" that will return our nation to its former glory.

The budget-balancing tax-cutting program is as follows:

1. Personnel

Cut the payroll of the federal government by one-third.

There are presently 2,050,000 federal employees, who cost us $161 billion a year, or $80,000 per person in cash for salaries, benefits, and pensions. This does not include the half-trillion dollars we owe the federal pension plan in unfunded monies.

We need to cut 675,000 federal workers over those seven years, which can be done by attrition without laying off a single person. Each year, 7 percent of the staff either retires, leaves, or dies—a total in this first year of 143,000 people. In descending order, by the end of the seventh year a total of 815,000 will have left by attrition. By hiring back 15 percent of the most essential workers, we reach our goal of 675,000 fewer government employees.

Examples of personnel waste: On a small scale, seventy workers in the Census Bureau count the population of *foreign* nations. In the Extension Service of the Department of Agriculture, 2,000 home economists no longer teach farmer's wives. Throughout the government, we have 4,000 publicists.

On a larger scale, we have one civilian employee for each two service personnel in the Defense Department. Not long ago it was one for three. During World War II, it was one for seven. Retain or increase the number of servicemen and cut 300,000 of the 850,000 civilian workers in the DOD.

The total personnel savings are large and direct: $54 billion annually by the year 2002.

(All figures are in today's dollars. They would be much higher in dollars of the year 2002.)

2. Federal Civilian Pensions

These are excessive and now cost us over $40 billion a year. They should be cut by 20 percent on the remaining personnel, eliminating such programs as matching the 5 percent of workers' salaries in a savings plan. COLAs, which start right at retirement, often at age fifty-five, should be delayed until true retirement, when workers go on Social Security or reach sixty-two. In addition, COLAs should be one-third less than inflation.

Retirees now receive health insurance, two-thirds of which is paid by the taxpayers. They should have access to the same health plan but pay for it themselves. That alone saves $4.5 billion a year.

Total savings by the year 2002, some $15 billion annually.

3. Overhead

The present overhead of the federal government seems to be a state secret.

"We've never done a study of overhead," says an official of the Office of Management and Budget.

But Congressman Lamar Smith of Texas has made "overhead" his hobby and has bedeviled the OMB to get the true figures, which has resulted in threats to throw his staff out of the OMB library.

"Our latest figures for 1995 show that the overhead is now $234 billion," says John Lampmann, chief of staff to Congressman Smith.

That, we might add, comes to an overhead of $115,000 per federal employee. When added to the cash only for salaries, benefits, and pensions, each federal employee costs the taxpayers $200,000—between two and three times the cost in private industry.

Although it's not highlighted anywhere in the budget, overhead is an enormous part of all government spending, covering such items as travel ($6.4 billion), moving of things ($5.3 billion), communications ($6.9 billion), consultants ($4.2 billion), rent, printing, and purchase of supplies and services.

There are also charming items like furniture and decorations ($1.3 billion), private planes (1,400 of them), cars (190,000), and computers, a multibillion-dollar operation with staggering maintenance costs.

Several of these plus other unlisted items, what others might call "miscellaneous," are covered in a catch-all budget disguise entitled "Other Services."

Now, how large could that be?

"Our latest research," says Mr. Lampmann, "indicates that 'Other Services' cost the taxpayers $139 billion in 1995."

New federal buildings keep piling on the overhead costs. Presently there are 105 buildings planned or going up, costing $8 billion—even though we are reducing manpower somewhat. One new building, at 13th and Pennsylvania Avenue, will end up costing almost a *billion* dollars alone. We need to place an immediate moratorium on all new buildings and cancel those now planned.

Congressman Lamar Smith is leading the charge to cut back on the $234 billion overhead. He has requested a simple 10 percent cut, which would save $23 billion a year toward deficit reduction or a tax saving.

"Many of the members of Congress we deal with have no idea how ridiculously wasteful this whole operation is," says Lampmann. "Anyone can save 10 percent if they try."

Of course, but they do not try, and I believe that heroic Mr. Smith is being kind to his colleagues.

With the one-third cut in personnel, we should easily be able to make a similar one-third cut in overhead by 2002.

The savings? Simple arithmetic—some $78 billion a year, almost half the entire deficit!

4. Useless Agencies

Over the years, the federal government has taken on agencies like Christmas tree decorations—pretty to look at but of little basic value, except to special interest groups.

Those agencies which should be phased out year by year until they are extinct by 2002 (in some cases much sooner) include:

RURAL ELECTRIFICATION ADMINISTRATION (Farms are virtually all electrified.)

INTERSTATE COMMERCE COMMISSION (Ninety-five percent of its duties are gone.)

APPALACHIAN REGIONAL COMMISSION (After thirty years, there's been no improvement in the relative income of the area.)

LEGAL SERVICES CORPORATION (A very expensive operation not available to the hard-pressed middle class.)

GOVERNMENT PRINTING OFFICE (Prices are double those of private printers.)

SMALL BUSINESS ADMINISTRATION (Loans each year to one in seven hundred small businesses, along with an enormous, expensive default rate.)

ECONOMIC DEVELOPMENT ADMINISTRATION (A true boondoggle.)

ESSENTIAL AIR (Subsidizes one hundred plane routes, including one from Washington to The Homestead, a $350-a-night hotel.)

U.S. INFORMATION AGENCY (The Cold War is over.)

COMMUNITY DEVELOPMENT BLOCK GRANTS (Another massive boondoggle costing over $4 billion a year. In my town, most of the money goes to United Way agencies.)

HELIUM RESERVE (Started in the 1920s to fill up blimps.)

EXPORT-IMPORT BANK (Agency admits to a 40 percent default on $15 billion a year in loans to foreigners.)

5. Job Training

There are presently over 150 job-training programs being operated in all fourteen cabinet agencies, from Food Stamp Job Training to Bureau of Reclamation Job Training.

Senator Nancy Kassebaum of Kansas, chairman of the Education and Labor Committee, puts its cost at $25 billion a year.

Close all of them except for one for adults and one for teenagers at the apprentice level. The latter is successfully run in Germany by the government in connection with the Chamber of Industry.

Give $10 billion in block grants to states for job training, with a mandate to install a high-school-to-corporation program.

Save $15 billion and do much better at job training, which is now mired in administration that takes almost half the money.

6. Cabinet Reform

After the Constitution was ratified, we had five cabinet agencies. Under Harry Truman, we had eight. Today we have fourteen going on fifteen (the EPA).

Close and consolidate the following cabinet agencies, leaving important duties to small, low-overhead, independent agencies. The cabinet offices involved include:

DEPARTMENT OF EDUCATION: Spends $31 billion a year and doesn't educate a single child, nor does it have any program that improves elementary and secondary education.

Chapter I, which spends $11 billion a year to help

disadvantaged children, is a failure by the Education Department's own standards. Replace it with young honor student tutors at minimum wage, operated by the states, who will receive a $4 billion grant.

Close the $7 billion Pell Grant program (poor children can take out student loans just as easily as middle-class children). Put student loans on a compulsory payback out of their salaries when they begin work, saving billions in defaults.

Close the Education Department and replace it with a small Office of Education (as it was before 1977), with a saving of $20 billion a year.

DEPARTMENT OF AGRICULTURE: This enormous agency, with 70,000 workers handling farming, is outdated. There are now more people in the computer business than in farming. (There are only 650,000 full-time significant farms.) Stop all farm subsidies and phase out the department, keeping only the valuable agricultural research and statistics in a small Office of Agriculture.

This enormously wasteful agency has 12,000 field offices throughout the nation. Mr. Clinton is cutting 1,200; the Senate is cutting 1,400. We should immediately close 6,000, and phase out the rest as the department starts to close.

DEPARTMENT OF LABOR and DEPARTMENT OF COMMERCE: Combine these two departments into a DEPARTMENT OF INDUSTRY AND LABOR. Shut down most of the functions except for statistical work and research and development aid. Fold what's left of AGRICULTURE into it, creating one cabinet agency named DEPARTMENT OF INDUSTRY, AGRICULTURE, AND LABOR.

DEPARTMENT OF ENERGY: Serves no real function. Give work on gas mileage to the EPA, and the nuclear activities to a revised Atomic Energy Commission.

DEPARTMENT OF TRANSPORTATION: This is a relatively new boondoggle whose main work should be divided back into two prior independent agencies, the Federal Highway Administration and the Federal Aviation Administration.

THE DEPARTMENT OF THE INTERIOR should become the DEPARTMENT OF NATURAL RESOURCES and absorb the U.S. Forest Service from Agriculture and some parts of the former Energy Department. Since Eastern states have few federal lands, there is no reason why Washington should own most of the West, which has become the major work of Interior.

The federal government, which owns 60 percent of California and over 90 percent of Alaska, should return most of that land (excluding the national parks) back to the states.

What are the savings?

Easily $50 billion a year by closing and realigning several cabinet agencies.

7. Medicaid

This program of medical care for the poor will pass $155 billion in cost in federal and state funds in fiscal 1995. The majority of the money is federal, but the rest (some $70 billion) puts great pressure on state budgets.

(Medicare, the health plan for the aged, can be streamlined somewhat since there is considerable provider fraud. But it operates much, much better than Medicaid.)

The Medicaid program contains at least 30 percent of waste. In Connecticut, for example, each person on Medicaid costs $2,700 (not counting more expensive nursing homes) or some $11,000 for a family of four.

National legislation should require an HMO for all recipients of Medicaid, which will save at least $20 billion a year.

In addition, overblown hospitals—with 35 percent empty beds—are over-fed by Medicaid funds. They charge hundreds of dollars to treat welfare patients for routine ailments in the emergency room. We need inexpensive pediatric clinics for children, who make up a majority of Medicaid patients.

Medicaid fraud is also rampant, says the FBI. It exists not only in medical care but in dentistry, an expensive program which is covered by Medicaid in forty-five states—a benefit not available to the aged, nor to most people with commercial health insurance plans.

Reforming and revamping Medicaid, including block grants to states, will save $50 billion a year, split between federal and state funds.

8. Pork

The waste peddled by egocentric congressmen seeking to get reelected by bringing home the bacon has to stop. A simple solution is to make it illegal for a member of any committee to assign additional money appropriated by his committee to anyone or anything in his home district, or to the home district of any other member of his committee. Horse trading between committees would be considered an ethical breach, punishable by the House and Senate.

Savings? There are no exact figures, but $8 billion a year is a reasonable estimate.

9. Welfare

According to the definitive report on welfare published by the Congressional Research Service (Vee Burke, author), there are eighty-one different welfare programs in the United States, run by six different cabinet agencies—Health and Human Services, Education, Labor, Energy, Agriculture, and Housing and Urban Development (HUD).

There is no central computer and no one, not even the president, could learn how many programs an individual or family is on, and how much they are receiving in cash and benefits. The cost, as of Fiscal 1992 (the report was published in 1993), was an astronomical $289 billion, three-fourths paid by the federal government and one-fourth by the states.

Today, that represents $384 billion a year in welfare benefits, from AFDC to Upward Bound to Food Stamps, Medicaid, housing vouchers, rural rental assistance, and an endless list of welfare programs—most of which are unknown to the American public.

There are two possible solutions, each with large savings:

(1) Cut out some fifty of the programs and consolidate the rest in a Department of Welfare, with one central computer.

(2) Close all eighty-one programs, except for the blind and disabled, and institute a national work program similar to the WPA (Works Progress Administration) started by FDR, which employed 5 million people during the Great Depression—equal to 10 million today.

Such work would draw a pay of $15,000 in higher-cost states and closer to minimum wage in poorer states. All WPA workers would receive an HMO health insurance policy, eliminating half the cost of Medicaid.

AFDC, housing, food stamps, etc., would be closed shut. Anyone who was not disabled and wanted federal aid would work for the WPA. The men would repair and build roads and bridges, rehabilitate the aging tenements, and construct day-care centers for the children. The women would work in the day-care centers (where they would bring their children), in schools as aides, in hospitals doing a variety of jobs.

The savings would be twofold in either plan—approximately $100 billion a year in funds, and a fortune in spiritual elevation, as the true sources of illegitimacy and family breakdown would be eliminated.

10. Corporate Welfare

The same failed welfare subsidies for the poor that are destroying them and bankrupting the nation, apply to government handouts to the corporate world as well.

Steven Moore of the Cato Institute has estimated that government "gifts" to business include some 125 programs that cost the Treasury some $85 billion a year. He lists Sematech, a consortium of chip makers that receives $100 million a year from Washington; farm subsidies that run from $8 billion to $20 billion a year; and road building in the U.S. forests that cost $140 million a year and enable wood products companies to come in and get cheap federal timber.

To that list we should add the Export-Import Bank loans; the Farmers Home Administration mortgage loans that have been as high as $50 billion, with an enormous default and forgiveness rate; the Pension Benefit Guaranty Corporation, which pays for the pensions of workers when corporations go belly-up; enormous overhead costs for research at universities; and many others.

All of this should be eliminated with the same sharp eye that we must use when looking at destructive welfare for the poor.

Savings? Some of it I have already recorded, but there's at least an additional $25 billion a year.

11. Overlap and Duplication

This is not a Washington law firm, but the ridiculous way the federal government does business. Each agency pretends it is the entire government and tries to do everything—with our money. For instance:

Twelve cabinet agencies are involved in education.
Twelve agencies handle the Indians.
Ten agencies deal with the environment.
Three agencies are involved in infant mortality work.
Fourteen cabinet agencies do job training.
Coastal waters are handled by four agencies.
Wetlands are supervised by five agencies.
Physical fitness is handled by five agencies.

The Congressional Budget Office looked at five new children's programs instituted in 1989, only a handful of scores of such projects in the government. They estimated that just coordinating those five under one bureaucratic umbrella would save $270 million a year.

All we need do is call on on a college computer hacker to construct a program that will assign one mission to one agency. The savings would probably be an additional $10 billion a year.

This is only a sampling of the reform and resulting savings in the federal operation. But this alone is enough to achieve the cuts necessary to balance the budget and bring in massive tax reduction each year until we reach the goal of a 25 percent cut across the board by 2002. (Once that's achieved, we should look at Washington again and see how much more waste can be eliminated.)

How can we make sure it happens?

To give such a program overall discipline on the yearly budget level, Congress should pass a ZERO GROWTH resolution, which, because of inflation, represents a real cut of 3.5 percent in the budget each year.

It's not very difficult. It requires only discipline and a sense of mission, something in insufficient supply in Washington today.

Now, having achieved a direct path to solvency, we should move on to our next objective: a better way to raise the money to run the smaller government.

Read on.

CLOSE THE IRS, PUT IN A NATIONAL SALES TAX, AND SAVE AMERICA

Why would a free people want to enslave themselves in the yoke of a complex income tax that requires both confession and confiscation of large portions of their income?

Why would a nation whose history was exemplary because of freedom from government snooping and punishment be willing to relinquish their sacred Bill of Rights protection in order to raise funds for a bloated government?

Why would a free people enslave themselves as compulsory bookkeepers for their own government, shivering nervously over every receipt and expenditure so that someday—under threat of enormous financial and personal grief—they might have to *prove* that they are actually honest citizens?

The answer is that they don't want such a coercive and punishing system and never had any intention of setting one up.

In the vernacular, it just "snuck" up on them when they weren't looking—when they were too busy working around the clock to pay those exorbitant taxes in the first place.

The perpetrators of this national crime are, of course, our politicians, for whom extortion of funds from families is a major occupation.

Their rationalization? It's twofold: (1) We can't let the rich get away with anything, and (2) many politicians come into office with unrealistic fantasy schemes of creating a Nirvana through government programs, especially for the poor, and are convinced that the pain inflicted on others through the income tax is worth the price.

The first excuse—soak the rich—was used in 1913 to amend the Constitution to permit income taxes, which had been outlawed in 1787. The second excuse is perpetual even though poverty rises as expenditures on welfare increase regularly.

Both rationalizations are, of course, false. There aren't enough rich to support the government, and the true burden, as we have seen, has fallen on the middle class. The poor (except for FICA) pay almost nothing into the income tax system.

Recent history shows that the psychological and financial burden of the IRS is for most people, a very new phenomenon. In 1950, only 2 percent of their earnings—a miscellaneous cost equal to clothing expenditures—went to federal income taxes. The erosion of our freedom and pocketbooks since then took place gradually over the years, each time with another false excuse conjured up by clever politicians.

Under Harry Truman, Washington was a faraway, inexpensive place for middle-class people. (The rich *were* being soaked.) The theater of politics was more important than the finances, because it all cost so little.

My, how times have changed. And with that change must come a new system of taxation.

The only viable substitute for the destructive IRS system is a national sales tax.

How would it work?

Quite simply. Right now, forty-five states have a sales tax system with a complete mechanism for collection. That tax is mainly on goods, although some states tax various services as well.

The national sales tax would use these same collection systems but add a tax on most services. What would be exempt? That's our first concern and the answer is simple.

Under the national sales tax, we would pay no taxes on food, housing, or medical care. Together, they make up some 40 percent of the budget of the typical family, and closer to 60 percent of the budget of poor families.

How much money do we have to raise to replicate the present IRS intake from taxes on individuals?

The 1994 figure for individual income taxes actually paid by Americans, according to the Office of Management and Budget, is $543 billion. This also includes the earnings of sole proprietors and capital gains taxes paid by individuals.

How are we going to raise that much money and what will the national sales tax rate be?

It's not difficult to calculate. The Gross Domestic Product in 1994 was $6.7 trillion and we will use that figure for our equation.

From that $6.7 trillion, we have to subtract the cost of food, housing, and medical care, which will not be taxed. According to Census Bureau figures, and exempting a good portion of business investment costs, that should leave us a national sales tax base of between $4 trillion and $4.2 trillion.

If we use the conservative number of $4.1 trillion, then we'll need a tax rate of only 13.5 percent to fully replace both the individual income tax receipts of $543 billion in 1994, and the $12 billion in inheritance taxes, which will also be eliminated.

Look at an example. If you buy a suit or a dress for $200, the national sales tax would be $27—a lot easier to take than April 15!

Who would do the collecting?

The same people who are now collecting state sales taxes, plus probably an additional one-third—people who provide services and who are now exempt in most states.

How can we be sure there would be no evasion?

We can't. Evasion is a historic part of the tax business in whatever form.

Right now, the IRS estimates that there is a "tax gap" of $127 billion, which is surely understated, especially considering the true criminal element, who file false or no returns. A $150 billion figure of missing income taxes would be conservative—and represents over one-quarter of all the individual taxes now collected.

But what of evasion in the national sales taxes—friends helping friends, barter, etc.?

Surely there will be some of that, but consider this:

Evaders will all continue to buy goods, whether cars or clothes or jewelry. Now, for the first time, they'll be paying full taxes!

It is my estimate that less than $50 billion will be lost through evasion, and that so much money will come in on the national sales taxes that we will be able to reduce the tax rate a little each year, perhaps reaching as low as 12 percent!

And I forgot. Research by Arthur D. Little and others indicates that billions of hours, costing at least $200 billion a year, are now spent in the tiresome preparation of income tax returns.

What about those millions of new collectors? Won't they mind the extra federal tax burden?

Perhaps. And they should be compensated for the extra effort. I believe we should allot one half of one percent (on a sliding scale), or some $3 billion, to compensate them.

To ensure that the money goes directly to Uncle Sam, retail and service people would be required to open *separate tax escrow accounts*. From their banks it would go directly to the National Sales Tax Office electronically after each deposit.

What about the poor?

That's the obvious and most-asked question. Aren't

they going to suffer, since they now pay so little in income taxes?

Provisions for that are simple. We can issue a refund for each person earning under a ceiling of, say, $25,000, phased in downward.

Since we do not want anyone to continue to file just to seek a refund, the simplest way is to reduce the employee's end of the FICA tax on each paycheck.

For example: If someone makes $15,000, and we presume that half of that is taxable (after food, housing, and medical care), then we would take 13.5 percent of $7,500, or a national sales tax of $1,013. That would be returned to them in the form of the FICA refund on each paycheck. As their income rises, the refund would be phased out.

I would estimate the cost of that at $50 billion a year. Where would it come from?

Simple. Either from the general fund, or better still, from the present FICA surplus of some $70 billion a year beginning in 1995. Since the government is now pilfering it for everything except Social Security, they'll just have less to play with.

But I have an even better suggestion, one which we might entertain. It will eliminate the need to refund money to the poor, and will free up everyone from any FICA deductions from their paycheck.

The idea is to take the employee's end of the FICA tax, which is now 7.65 percent (including Medicare hospitalization), and, as Senator Moynihan has suggested, eliminate the false surplus by cutting it back by 20 percent. Then the true pay-as-you-go FICA tax, the employee's end would only be 6.12 percent, about where it used to be.

ADD THAT 6 PERCENT TO THE 13.5 PERCENT. ROUND IT OUT AND INSTITUTE A 20 PERCENT NATIONAL SALES TAX.

Not only income taxes, but Social Security and Medicare taxes for individuals would also become a thing of the past!

(Employers would continue to pay their share of FICA to ensure that there will be enough money in the fund.)

That 6 percent, along with the employer's payroll share, would go into the new independent Social Security fund, which, free of Washington control, would be invested to build a real retirement for the baby boomers, and their children, and their children's children.

Everyone, including the self-employed, would be covered under this new sales-tax-supported Social Security plan.

Again, what about the poor? Under that plan, they'd make out like fiscal bandits. A person now making $20,000, for example, is paying the most regressive tax in Western history—7.65 percent from the *first* dollar earned, or $1,430 a year. With a 20 percent national sales tax, he would—as would we all—receive his full paycheck for the first time in modern history.

Just the savings of FICA would more than offset any national sales taxes he would have to pay, plus a nice profit.

What are the benefits of the new system, psychologically and financially?

- No more bookkeeping by individuals.
- No more filing.
- A savings rate which will double, even triple, within a year.
- A sharp drop in interest rates.
- $100 billion saved on evasion.
- Those who now evade taxes will pay when they buy.
- $200 billion saved on tax preparation.
- You become the major controller of what you pay in taxes.
- Eliminates the entire tax code with its thousands of complex codiciles.
- Eliminates the double taxation of dividends. (As the economy grows with the end of the IRS, we would try to phase out corporate taxes as well.)
- Stops the so-called progressive tax penalty against success.
- Eliminates the capital gains tax and opens new investment possibilities.
- Eliminates the inheritance tax.
- No more audits, penalties, interest, levies, liens, threats, and seizures.
- NO MORE APRIL 15.

Perhaps the most important gain to the body politic is philosophical. It will restore some of our lost faith in government and free us from the increasing fear that we are all becoming vassals, rather than masters, of Washington.

Never in our history have we had such an opportunity to sharply reverse a destructive trend in American civilization. It can be accomplished by the implementation of this single idea: the closing of the IRS and its replacement with a national sales tax, one which is painless, visible, and viable.

To all who love their country, I heartily commend this plan and hope that it will become a reality by the year 2000. Then in unison, we can all happily chant:

FREE AT LAST! FREE AT LAST!

THE GROSS TAX TEST:
FIGURE YOUR REAL TAX BILL!

TAX	DESCRIPTION	YOUR TAX
Airline and Airport Taxes	Add up domestic airline tickets for your family and take 10 percent. On international flights, add $25 per person per flight.	
Bridge and Highway Tolls	Figure all tolls, including commuting. Add tolls paid on vacation as well.	
Capital Gains Tax	Did you pay any last year? Add that up.	
County Taxes	Check property tax bill. County may be listed separately.	
Dividend Taxes	List all dividends. One tax is already on the 1040. For first tax at source, take 52 percent of the amount.	
Environmental Taxes	If you recycle home garbage, add $50 a year for extra fee.	
Excise Taxes	Take 10 percent average on guns, fishing rods, etc. Also add boat taxes and fees. For cruise, take $3 per person. Check gas guzzler tax on large cars.	
Federal Income Tax	Check your 1040 and list amount here. If married and filing separately, add the two together.	
Gambling Taxes	Any W2-Gs, or other confession to Uncle Sam, on gaming winnings?	
Gasoline Tax	Take 40 cents a gallon on average, or $400 for 16,000 miles. If you drive more, increase proportionately.	

SUBTOTAL _____

TAX	DESCRIPTION	YOUR TAX
Hotel and Travel Taxes	Add up hotel and car rental bills, then take a 13 percent average.	
Income Tax, State and City	Check last year's returns. List them and weep.	
Inheritance Taxes	Did you inherit any money? If so, take about 45 percent as taxes paid before you got it.	
Junk Food Tax	Sweet-tooth tax best figured with sales tax.	
License Tax	List car license and registration fees. If professional or occupational license, add that.	
Luxury Tax	Take 10 percent of any car purchase over $32,000.	
Marriage Tax	You're paying, but it's built into your federal and state income taxes.	
Options, Stock, and Bond Taxes	Get out all your slips and add up the SEC fee.	
Parking and Garage Taxes	Estimate money put in parking meters, then add any municipal tax on garaging (18 percent in New York).	
Penalties and Interest	Any special dealings with the IRS? Add these up. Same with state or city.	
Personal Property Tax	List yearly car tax. Add any other PPT on computers, etc.	
Personal Property (Intangible) Tax	Residents of Florida, Georgia, etc., list amount. Others check their state tax on this.	

SUBTOTAL _____

TAX	DESCRIPTION	YOUR TAX
Real Estate (Home Property) Tax	List total here (plus any interest) or breakup of tax as indicated—town, county, schools, etc.	
Sales Tax	List car tax or other big-ticket item. Then take 20 percent of income and multiply by your sales tax rate. A family with $65,000 income would come to about $780 extra.	
School Taxes	Generally the largest part of your property tax, about $3,000 on a $5,000 bill.	
Self-Employed Taxes	Look at the FICA tax on your 1040. First weep, then enter it.	
Sin Taxes	The price of all wine and liquor times 40 percent. Cigarettes, figure fifty cents a pack. On beer, take an average of seventy-seven cents per six-pack.	
Small Business Taxes	In New York City and elsewhere, list Unincorporated Business Tax. Otherwise, ask your accountant.	
Social Security Taxes	FICA tax amount for employees is on your 1040. This is a big one.	
Telephone and Cable Taxes	Five percent of yearly cable bill. Add $42 for each phone number in home, plus 3 percent of your yearly phone bill.	

TOTAL _____

ADD IT ALL UP—AND GOOD LUCK!

APPENDIX

The following organizations are working to improve America's tax system and are in favor of reducing the burden on taxpayers. They will be happy to give you additional information on the entire question of taxation and/or the need for smaller government. They include:

Citizens for an Alternative Tax System
National Office
9401 East Street
Manassas, Virginia 22110
800-767-7577

National Taxpayers Union
325 Pennsylvania Avenue, S.E.
Washington, D.C. 20003
202-543-1300

Tax Foundation
1250 H Street, N.W.
Suite 750
Washington, D.C. 20005-3908
202-863-5454

Cato Institute
1000 Massachusetts Avenue, N.W.
Washington, D.C. 20001-5403
202-842-0200

Citizens for a Sound Economy
1250 H Street, N.W.
Washington, D.C. 20005-3908
202-783-3870

National Center for Policy Analysis
3420 E. Shea Blvd.
Suite 226
Phoenix, Arizona 85028
214-386-6272

Americans for Tax Reform
1301 Connecticut Avenue, N.W.
Suite 444
Washington, D.C. 20036
202-785-0266

Small Business Survival Committee
1320 18th Street, N.W.
Washington, D.C. 20036
202-785-0238

Competitive Enterprise Institute
1001 Connecticut Avenue, N.W.
Suite 1250
Washington, D.C. 20036
202-331-1010

Citizens Against Government Waste
1301 Connecticut Avenue, N.W.
Washington, D.C. 20036
202-467-5300

National Federation of Independent Business
600 Maryland Avenue, S.W.
Washington, D.C. 20024
202-554-9000

**Institute for Research on the Economics of Taxation
(IRET)**
1300 19th Street, N.W.
Suite 240
Washington, D.C. 20036
202-463-1400

ABOUT THE AUTHOR

The Tax Racket: Government Extortion From A to Z is the seventh nonfiction work of author, editor, and educator Martin L. Gross.

It follows the publication of his phenomenal bestsellers *The Government Racket: Washington Waste from A to Z* and *A Call for Revolution*, which triggered a national debate on the subject of government spending, inefficiency, and the need for true change.

Both books were *New York Times* bestsellers for more than thirty weeks and *The Government Racket* reached the No. 1 position on the *Washington Post* list.

Mr. Gross is also the author of *The Great Whitewater Fiasco*, published in 1994.

Mr. Gross has appeared on a host of national television shows including "Larry King Live," "Good Morning America," "20/20," "CBS This Morning," "Prime Time Live," "The Tom Snyder Show," CNN, and C-Span to share his investigative research.

The author has testified before the U.S. Senate and the House of Representatives five times on the subject of waste and inefficiency in government, and has recommended many cuts to balance the budget. He has also received thanks from the vice president's office for his revelations, several of which were used in the *National Performance Review*.

Ross Perot has called his work a "handbook for cleaning out the stables" of federal government. He has also been praised by former Senator William Proxmire and many other public figures.

The former editor of *Book Digest* magazine, Mr. Gross is an experienced reporter who covered Washington for many years for national publications. His syndicated column, "The Social Critic," appeared in newspapers throughout the country, including the *Los Angeles Times*, *Newsday*, and the *Chicago Sun-Times*. His articles have been published in a variety of magazines, from *Life* to *The New Republic*.

The author's prior nonfiction works, including *The Brain Watchers*, *The Doctors*, and *The Psychological Society*, were selections of major book clubs and aroused significant controversy.

Mr. Gross served on the faculty of the New School for Social Research for many years and has been Adjunct Associate Professor of Social Science at New York University.